PURSUING A HEAVENLY VISION

PURSUING A HEAVENLY VISION

STEWART KEILLER

Terra Nova Publications

Published in Great Britain by
Terra Nova Publications International Ltd.
Orders and enquiries: PO Box 2400 Bradford on Avon BA15 2YN
Registered Office (not for trade): 21 St.Thomas Street, Bristol BS1 6JS

Cover design by Joel Freeborn

ISBN 978 1 901949 57 5

Printed in Great Britain by
Creative Print and Design Group, Harmondsworth

Contents

Dedication

In the service of the King
extending his kingdom

FOREWORD

Some years ago I heard the Lord Jesus say to me that many were soon going to be entering into the 'holiness of realized destiny'. I did not have a clue as to what he was really saying. As I pursued this I soon began to understand that in God's thinking holiness is far more than simply the absence of sin in one's life. Biblical holiness is to embrace three things — the person of God, the ways of God, and the specific will of God for each of our lives.

Since that time there have come about many good messages and books on the topics of destiny, vision, purpose, etc. In fact, there is almost a glut of them on the market. What makes me excited about *Pursuing a Heavenly Vision* by Stewart Keiller, however, is that Stewart's message is relating vision and destiny within the context of the Father's love and the Spirit of God's voice.

God is incredibly specific in everything he does. And that includes his creating of each of us. God's word, in

Psalm 139, along with Genesis 1, tells us that even in our mother's womb God's hand was upon us to create a unique and specific reflection of himself. God is no paint by numbers artist. He never creates round pegs to simply comply and modify so that they be forced through a square hole. He creates us to be unique in Christ and to be uniquely gifted in Christ. As well, and why we need Stewart's message, is because his destiny and vision for each of us is unique.

That unique vision God has for each of us, however, is not found in any manual. It cannot be achieved by trying to wear someone else's armour as King David realized. It can only be heard, seen, and realized in the context of the Father's love and leading. Too many people, both non Christian and Christian, are attempting to plan and strategize their lives out of someone else's dream and/or vision. True happiness can only be realized by being right with God and being right in his specific will for each of us. The Bible tells us that Jesus himself said that his 'meat' – what fed and nourished him – was doing the specific will of the Father for his life.

In addition to teaching on destiny and vision there has also been a great deal taught, written, and ministered about the Father heart of God in recent years. This has been of great importance as so much of humanity is growing up without any sense of security or significance derived from parental love. However, much of the current

Father heart teaching focuses on the foundation of the Father's love but seldom goes on to touch on doing the Father's will. Jesus, knowing that he had come from the Father and was going back to the Father (John 13:3), was free to walk not only in the Father's love, but also in his complete will. Stewart is to be thanked for teaching us that the vision God has for us comes from a loving and deeply caring God.

I have had the privilege of knowing Stewart for several years. As well, I have been privileged to minister alongside him in his home church in Bath, England. I can truly say that Stewart not only has a great heart for people to know God's great love, but also for people to enter into the amazing adventure God has created for each of us. I am glad to say this is not just 'another good vision' book, but it will prove to be a key tool for many to come into the joy of knowing God's unique purposes for their lives!

Marc A. Dupont
Mantle of Praise Ministries, Inc.

One

HEAVENLY INSPIRED

When I hear an inspirational piece of oratory, something inside me tingles. Creating a vision statement is now an essential part of most companies and organisations. Why? Because without clarity of vision, failure is the inevitable consequence. Vision is about letting people 'see' something with their hearts and minds, something that is currently not a reality, but can become a reality.

The human journey is littered with notable people with vision; whether we think of a romantic poet or a world-class scientist; a motivating passionate vision seems to be evident in the person who achieves an action which ends up in the history books. As believers we are no different. We need to get hold of something that will motivate and inspire us. But unlike people without faith we need to get 'sight' of the Father. Without a vision of the Father we inevitably fix our eyes on something else, and because it is not heavenly in origin it will fade or probably fail. Vision is about setting our goals, aspirations and plans on an end that will not fail, tire, fade or fizzle out. Let's lift our eyes not to what *we* can do, not to what a great preacher can do, but to what the Father can do, will do and is doing.

WITHOUT A VISION, THE PEOPLE PERISH

When there is no vision we fall over, get worn out and tired. The Bible puts it this way: *Where there is no vision [no redemptive revelation of God], the people perish* (Proverbs 29:18, AMP).

Having a vision – or clear revelation – is key to us keeping on track. Without the release of clear vision we are trapped in a cycle, we raise expectations, work hard, but don't achieve what we hope for. The book of Proverbs says, *Hope deferred makes the heart sick* (Proverbs 13:12, NIV). We are not created to continually defer that which is promised; delay produces disillusionment and disappointment.

Many employers know this cycle at work in their organisations. It is why major corporations invest in training and development; they are looking to exploit the potential in the individual. However, companies are also aware that if they raise the expectations of the individual and fail to meet them then they will inevitably lose them to a competitor. How many of us reading this have been in a job which failed to meet our expectations? What were the consequences? We looked around for another job as soon as we were bored.

VISIONS THAT FAIL
(OR SEEM TO)

I used to be an employer's nightmare! Having a very low boredom threshold, I needed to find a new challenge every twelve to eighteen months. When, finally, I became an employer in my own business, this cycle was a major problem. I would invest myself, skills and training into a person, which in turn raised their expectations, only to disappoint them because I could not deliver what they wanted.

The cycle works in the church. I am sure many of us will recognise our excitement at being part of a church that is going somewhere. Perhaps we are recognised by the leaders; perhaps we put ourselves through some intensive discipleship training course; we sit on the front row, praise with great enthusiasm and have a sign on our heads that reads, 'ready to be used'. Perhaps we are young and full of promise, fresh out of college or university, or have just finished some ministry training programme. We feel that we are God's gift to the church and let everyone know it.

I remember the occasion when Deborah (my wife) and I were called to move from Winchester to the city of Bath. We were newly married, enthusiastic believers, just graduated. God gave me a dream that we should move from the church where we had met while at university, and go to Bath. He had also been talking to Deborah, and so with youthful, simple faith we started the process of talking to leaders and friends to confirm God's word to us and then made steps to move into what we felt God had spoken to us.

Well, things all came together very easily. We sold our house privately, got relocated by my employer, had a pay rise and a company car, and managed to buy a house in Bath after one weekend visit! So by the time we arrived at the church, we knew God was calling us to join. I was totally convinced that we were not only going to join the 'eldership' immediately, these people must have been praying for us to arrive! I remember feeling full of the call of God walking into the 'introduction' course for new members, expecting everyone in the room to stop, look and then say, 'Hallelujah, you are here! We have been waiting for you.' Of course, none of that happened; in fact it was the sort of church that seemed to have everything sorted out! 'So why exactly, Father God, did you want us to come here?' It took eighteen years until God's plans became clearer!

Well there is a cycle at work. I got a vision – I acted upon the vision – I got disappointed – vision faded.

A PICTURE FROM HEAVEN

As believers we should be filled with a vision that is not a promise of something vague or a hope that 'one day' you will realise it. Vision should cast a picture that we can grasp and make happen. A 'heavenly inspired' vision may paint a difficult picture; it may raise obstacles that seem like mountains in our sight; a heavenly sent vision may even look like an outrageous impossibility; but once you have grasped this sort of vision you feel you can scale any obstacle!

I am convinced that Father God is calling the church to take a higher view at this time. We must change our attitudes so that we don't present a vision of something that we expect to happen tomorrow. Vision should be about taking the long view. Yet so often we go along with what our culture demands —quick fixes. We have to come up higher, which we would do if only we took a God view on life. We should not live like the 100m sprinter, expending a quick burst of energy for a race that lasts only a moment. Instead, we must take the long-distance runner's view, keeping the whole course in mind and running according to the route that is marked out. Take the long view and run the race in the kingdom, building for the future. Vision should give you the long view, it must give us God's view. The Western church is full of disappointed Christians who have been fed short term vision. The consequence is that they have become sick in their spirits because church feels like a bit of an empty promise.

'Come up higher' is the word of God to us at this time. Are we prepared and expectant to go to a higher place and look at our lives the way Father sees them? If enough of us learn to position ourselves to take a higher look, we will never want to go back down and embrace an 'earthly' perspective. When we begin to be aware of how God sees things, we achieve a totally different view. It is like walking up a mountain or hill: it is pretty tough climbing, but as you get to the top, what a view! —amazing; always worth the effort. The church needs to get God's view on life, history, politics, the church, sin, power, healing. For just about anything and everything in the sphere of mankind, there is a perspective in heaven for us to have a look at. The trouble is that so few of God's children bother to visit Father.

SEEING WHAT FATHER IS DOING

Jesus continually took the high view on his life. *Jesus gave them this answer: "I tell you the truth, the Son can do nothing by himself; he can do only what he sees his Father doing, because whatever the Father does the Son also does."* (John 5:19, NIV)

Jesus did not let the issues of life control his self-image or destiny, rather he saw what the Father was up to, and then did what he saw, with amazing results. Isn't it cute when a three-year-old imitates what Dad is up to? Dad washes the car and the child has a sponge to help too. That is what we are supposed to do —copy the Father. How do we get to the Father? Through the Son, empowered by the Holy Spirit.

Why do we all stay down here taking an immediate, earthly view? We have a permanent invitation to see it from God's perspective. Jesus said that he was going back to the Father so that we could have a way to get up there too. He said that there wasn't any other way, just through him. Jesus has made a way to go up there. Have you ever noticed when you feel really low, the best thing you can do is go to a high place and look down? Everything falls into place when you change your perspective. So don't stay with an 'earth-bound' perspective — get a heavenly perspective. 'Come up here and see it from my place,' says your Father!

Being on earth is not some sort of punishment, you know. God created earth and mankind for a relationship with him. It is designed to be a place where God can dwell and inhabit, where he can make his home. Earth was always designed to be a bit of a holiday home! God's permanent dwelling is in heaven, but he made earth to enjoy as well. That is why each Christian is a living stone, a piece of the temple; we are a piece of something else, a piece of something much bigger. It is just that 'sin problem' — it seems to stop Father visiting! Well, have no fear. God has sorted out the sin problem; it really is not a problem any more; it is sorted and can be dealt with. That means that God will once again inhabit and dwell on earth. Yes, there is rubbish all around, it is not as clean as God created it, but it will all be taken care of —and ultimately there will be a new heaven and a new earth. *So we fix our eyes not on what is seen, but on what is unseen. For what is seen is temporary, but what is unseen is eternal* (2 Corinthians 4:18, NIV). *Let us fix our eyes on Jesus, the author and perfecter of our faith . . .* (Hebrews 12:2, NIV).

Fix your eyes on things above. Not enough of us are looking up to him. But don't stay looking up gazing into the stars, hoping for that final return, longing for something to happen that will whisk you away. Get up into the heavenly realms and have a look for yourself. In God's house there is an apartment, room, mansion or house for every single one of us. Don't leave it all for the day you die to have a look at it, get up there and take a look. We need to renew our imagination and see what God is up to.

Jesus said that he only did what he saw the Father doing. Okay, how did he see it? How did Jesus do that? Jesus was a man like us; he had all the temptations, all the issues that trip up any man, except he didn't fall for them. Why? Because he was God? No, that's not the answer. Jesus dwelt with the Father and saw what the Father was up to. Even as a young boy he was in the temple (God's house) and couldn't understand why his human parents didn't know where to find him. He was a man who knew where his Father was. He asked the Father stuff, saw him in action and learned from him. Jesus laid aside his special position to live life the way that it can be lived. That is, sin free, operating in total authority, in the overflow of heaven, knowing how to access all that is in heaven on earth. Jesus never had a problem with lack, never had an issue with a demon that wouldn't budge, he never met a sickness that wouldn't be healed. He lived on God's side of the fence and walked on earth in the power that he accessed from heaven.

If our vision for our lives is constrained and moulded by our earthly surroundings we will never realise the heavenly opportunities waiting for us. If heaven is something that only becomes real when we die then we have seriously missed the point. Heaven should be the source of our inspiration, the spring of our creativity and the pacemaker that marks our time on earth. A heavenly inspired vision in our lives will release a body of believers who can and will see his will done on earth, as it is in heaven.

Two

FINDING YOUR LIFE VISION

I have been involved in setting up a number of businesses over the years, and it always starts with an idea. It doesn't have to be an amazing radical idea, just an idea. The team that I work with now have got used to my hare-brained plans. Most of the ideas never get beyond being just ideas, and admittedly most of them should stay as an idea, for they would never work! However, every so often one of these ideas escapes from its nest in my mind; it so grips me that I feel that I just have to go for it. For a time the idea is all consuming, I work it over in my mind until it is ready to be tested by those around me. Normally, the first test is my wife who asks me those awkward questions: Who? What? Why? When? Where? How???!!! I try to refrain from sharing my latest scheme to avoid her simple but incisive scrutiny until absolutely necessary, and then will try all manner of emotional tactics to make her feel guilty for asking me the 'what are you talking about' question. Her questions can come like a massive hurricane hitting the idea. The idea either runs for cover, or it stands its ground. It is not that I have all the answers to the barrage of questions, but rather the fledgling idea has passed the first test.

STARTING WITH AN IDEA

All of us, from time to time, have had an idea or a dream. Man is made to have ideas. Take Adam in the garden of Eden. God gives him the task to name every living creature. He brings each creature to Adam and he has to name them. I am sure that this seemed quite a good game at first to Adam – 'Ah, rhinoceros, and how about monkey . . . and slug, that seems appropriate . . . get a move on slug . . . .' Whenever I am in a group of people and we have to come up with a name for a project or event it goes very quiet. Then someone will come up with a name that is totally inappropriate and you want to say, 'Oh, don't be so stupid', but out comes, 'Well, that's a good idea, any others?' I don't know whether Adam got a bit bored with the 'name game' but it caused him to go into a deep sleep!

Ideas are not enough. They are the starting point, but in themselves they are not enough. Anybody who has had a business idea will tell you that from this starting point it very quickly has to turn into something with substance, something that can actually happen, a viable proposition. When dealing with something that God lays on your heart there will always be substance to the idea. If an idea has its origin from heavenly places then it is something that is not a wacky dream, but rather a rock-solid dependable concept that will go all the way. Heaven is a place where moth and rust do not destroy (see Matthew 6:19), where the operating system is faith, which is something of substance (Hebrews 11:1, AV).

LOOK AT YOURSELF!

A good place to start the pursuit of vision is by having a long sober look at yourself. Ask yourself what type of person you are, what do you like, what are you gifted at? Have a look at your circumstances and time of life. Now I say this not to limit any of us — not at all. It is good to judge ourselves soberly so that when God speaks we have appraised ourselves. I find it amazing how many people really don't know who they are or what they are made to be. We are described as parts of a body made to function together,[1] so it would be helpful, if we are to function with other parts, to get an understanding of the part that we are.

DIGGING UP OLD DREAMS

What has God told you in the past? What idea and thought did you hear when you were younger that you have just filed away under 'never going to happen'? Perhaps we heard God speak to us years ago, when we were young; we got excited about some way in which Father was going to use us. Perhaps we have dismissed some dream as just being a nice story, that we can tell to our grandchildren, 'Oh I wanted to do that when I was younger'. May I suggest that you get digging. Why not dig up some of those old fancies and thoughts and see if they have the life and substance of heaven in them. Sure, many may have been birthed out of ambition or motives that you are now suspicious of. Many of the old dreams may well be better dead and buried because they never had the breath of God on them. But maybe, just maybe they were God speaking to you and revealing his heart and purposes to you, but for whatever reason you didn't believe him or take him at his word. Just perhaps there is life in those dreams still.

One of my daughters was given a small notebook one Christmas which had on it the words 'Brilliant Ideas' – well get your version of that out and have a look. If you haven't got one then may I suggest you go out tomorrow and buy an empty notebook, write on the outside 'brilliant ideas' and go on a journey with your Father in heaven and write down the most amazing ideas!

RECALLING THE PROMISES OF GOD

When God speaks he means what he says. The whole of the visible and invisible spheres came about by a word. The *let there be . . .* in Genesis is all about creating something from nothing. The void gives way to created substance all because God spoke! God's promises are incredibly powerful because they are of course his word.

Abraham's wife, Sarah, is credited in Hebrews with faith, believing God would do what was promised.[2] But when you actually read the story in Genesis it is not as if she was some courageous faith-filled woman of destiny —no, she laughed![3] We find the Lord, and two others, appearing – apparently physically – to Abraham, by the orchard in Mamre. Abraham, who we assume is having a siesta, jumps to his feet and insists that the visitors have some water. (Similar to the British response at times of emergency, or when we have an unexpected visitor – give them a cup of tea!) The visitors ask about Abraham's wife, who is listening on the other side of the tent door, and proceed to make a promise that she will have a son! Just be polite to the visitor —what does he know? Mrs A is naturally grandmother material, not a first time mum. No wonder she 'laughed within herself'. The Lord hears Sarah muttering and realises that she is mocking him, "Is anything too hard for the Lord?" – well, that put her in her place. She strenuously denied laughing, but of course she did. It was doubly amusing because Abraham also laughed with derision before God when he was told that he was going to have a baby.[4] Sometimes even the promises of Jehovah God seem utterly ridiculous!

I can imagine that this episode lived with Sarah for a good number of years afterwards. She must have thought about the promise that the Lord made to her. Perhaps she was tempted to laugh again, but then I think that she remembered how uncomfortable she felt the first time her inner thoughts were discovered. After all, the words, 'Is anything too hard for the Lord?' have a resonance that is difficult to forget. A few chapters later, after Abraham tries to pass off his wife as his sister to get him out of a scrape, the Lord visits Sarah and, 'did for Sarah as he had spoken.'[5] Appropriately, they call the child 'laughter' (Isaac) because of their mocking laughter which is now turned into laughter of joy.

But despite Sarah's mocking laughter, God does not hold it against her, but remembers (in Hebrews) her as a woman that held to the promise of God and believed. You know it is not too late to recall the promise of God in your life. You may have laughed at the promise the first time, thought what God was asking you to do totally ridiculous, but actually it is a promise that you can dust down and choose to believe.

LETTING DESTINY HAPPEN

You may have heard endless sermons about God's destiny and plan for your life, but you know it's true! There is a heap of good things that Father wants to do in your life; all you have to do is line up your thinking with his thinking and start 'in faith' to walk it out. Your destiny isn't a foregone conclusion that will automatically happen —we do have a choice in the matter. I don't think it worthwhile to get into the theological debate about predestination and free will in this book, rather let's just settle on the conclusion that God created us with free will that enables us to choose his plan for our lives, or reject it. It is true of when we first believe, it is also true of how we choose to live our lives. You have a list of unfulfilled promises over your life, why not ask the Father one relevant one for today? It is quite easy really, just settle yourself in the Spirit, tune into God's voice and hear what he has to say to you. Let him talk to you about your destiny, about his plans for you, *plans to prosper you and not to harm you.*[6] Don't be too concerned if you get stuff that you like or have felt before —it is likely that God has spoken things into your spirit before; it is equally likely that he wants you to do things that you want to do. When I am trying to get something done, I try to find someone whose passions and interests line up with what I want done. Over the years I have realised that there is no point in giving someone a task to do if they are reluctant, even if I think it is good for them. Instead I find people who are passionate about the project that I want to be completed, even if they are not as skilled as someone less passionate. I think God is a bit like that when he gives out jobs. Why do our minds instantly think that if God is allocating dreams and desires we are going to be the ones landed with being 'missionaries'! God wants us to be fulfilled, he knows what we want and wants to give us the desires of our heart.[7] Sure, there are times when Father wants us to do something to which our instant reaction is 'yuk', but my experience is that something happens to our reactions to make doing his will a delight and not a chore.

There is a massive destiny for you, and it is not automatically going to happen whatever you do. In fact, the choices you make will have a bearing on whether you move into your destiny and how quickly you do so. But if you seek God, living your life listening to him and doing what he tells you, then you will fulfil your destiny – that's a promise!

LETTING YOUR HEART BE MOVED

Not everyone seems to have a massive appointment with their destiny. We don't all have clear-cut promises guiding us and shaping our lives. Sometimes our 'life vision' is formed as we respond to the events we encounter in a particular moment.

This can often be seen in the world around us. Many are moved by the terrible sufferings of others, and some have the vision and motivation to do something about those problems, seeking to help people by practical action.

In the Bible we see Nehemiah as a man who was moved by events and by God. He was a government minister in the Persian court of Artaxerxes.[8] He was an Israelite by descent, but trained and cultured in the sophisticated ways of Persia. He manages to meet up with some Jews who have returned from his beloved homeland, a mere obscure outpost of the empire, and quizzes them as to the state of the Jews who have survived the captivity, and as to the state of the city itself. By all accounts the reports were grim; there was great distress, and the all-important city walls, which kept the city's integrity and security, were broken down and the gates had been burned to the ground. Not the news he was hoping for. His response was mourning, fasting, weeping and praying. Something moved him to pray deeply, the sort of prayer that comes from the depths of your being, cutting into the spiritual atmosphere. Nehemiah was repentant and prayed for an opportunity to go before the king.

Well, the time comes for wine to be served and the king notices how glum Nehemiah is. The king recognises that Nehemiah is sad to the core of his being and gives him an opportunity to speak. These were days when you could be executed on the spot for speaking out of turn; this was not just a matter of etiquette but life or death. "Well, it's like this," Nehemiah blurts out, "my home town is a wasteland, the city gates have been burnt down." It's out in the open; call the executioner! 'What do you want then?' What was that? A quick prayer – 'Um, could you send me to Judah so that I can start repairing it?'

Now the king was going to flip completely! 'Okay.' What! Nehemiah pressed in and ended up with visas for the territories that he would have to travel through, and unlimited access to free supplies from the state-owned builders' merchants. This was a good day for him to open his mouth.

Nehemiah did not get visited by an angel, did not have a dream, did not hear the voice of the Lord – he responded to the tale of a few unknown Jewish migrants and allowed his heart to be moved by what he heard. Your heavenly vision may not come with a dramatic revelation, you may just have your heart pulled on by events. But was your vision birthed in God? Absolutely! I am reminded of Jesus who was 'moved with compassion' and healed many.[9] He didn't need a specific word from God to go and heal someone, he was moved. There is much that the church needs to go and do out of compassion. When it came to responding to the homeless in my home town, I didn't have to be convinced that this was God's plan and God's heart – of course responding to the needs of the most vulnerable is the Father's heart. Sure we need to pray about the specifics, but our response to the need, our determination to do something, needs action.

TAKE CLEAR STEPS

Let's get very practical. Vision can be all waffle and airy-fairy if you are not careful. Vision, in order to be workable, needs to be grounded. We need the lofty phrases, but they must be rooted in firm positive action. When Nehemiah got the OK he didn't pussyfoot around, he got on with it. Please don't get all vague when you have got an idea about what it is that God has given you, get very practical and very clear. If you are not clear, then you will be in exactly the same place in a year's time, nothing will have changed, you will be adding another dream to your store of dreams that you have let go of.

SUBMIT TO FATHER

I love that line in Nehemiah after he is asked by the king, 'What do you request?'[10] —the response, 'So I prayed to the God of heaven.' We may have heard from God and are clear, but we need to be a people who submit our plans to the Lord time and time again. My instinct is always to get on with it, but I am so aware that I may know God's heart for something but need to get the right tactics to implement it. We are promised success if we commit to God whatever we do,[11] so at the start of our adventures we need to be humble in heart before God and let him tell us if our plans need correcting. We are to commit to God whatever we do. Praying does not mean there is to be inactivity. We are to commit what we do; there may have to be 'doing' in order for us to commit. My own experience is that God seldom will rearrange events unless there is an action on our part. I have found that when I give generously according to his word, God does provide for my needs. Faith often requires action. You know when you get a new credit card it will sometimes have a sticker on it that says that before you can use the card you need to call a number – well sometimes it is a bit like that with God —he sometimes lets you know there is a step you need to take, and then he will come through for you, and provide all that you need. The major difference is, of course, that with any true vision, in his sovereignty he gave you the vision in the first place.

TESTING THE PASSION

Now before you run off and pursue a vision so grand and so adventurous in design I would just like to give a few checks and balances (phew, I hear all the pastors cry).

When we are given heaven-birthed vision we need to share our journey and passion with those we are accountable to. Normally this will be your local church leadership. Although I love to give people room to 'have a go', the church is not a very comfortable place for the maverick who will just go and do what they want to do regardless of anyone else. If God has put a burning passion in you, that will be evident to your church leaders, so talk to them and let their wisdom help shape the vision you have been given.

You may get confirmation from a number of sources: from the Bible, from prophetic words, from a dream. When you get these confirmations, write them down. If you are anything like me you will forget them fairly quickly after receiving them. That doesn't make them unimportant, it just means that your memory isn't photographic! You will find that over time you will collect many of these words and at some time you will need to step out on the basis of them. Please don't get to ninety years of age and have a journal full of the words that God has given you without having stepped out on them. Perhaps the Father is repeating the same message again and again because he wants you to do something about it. But time has a habit of confirming a word to you. Many of the really heavenly inspired words will seem totally impossible to do anything about and need some time to line up to make them realisable.

As we teach our prophetic people, 'timing is everything'. You may have a great vision and need to take steps to go for it, but you may have the timing a bit off. Please don't assume that because you have heard words now it will all happen now. We have to hold them before God and allow him to focus us on the timing of what he wants. Hence the reason to follow the proverb, 'commit to the Lord whatever you do', because as we move in on the vision we need to be clear about the next step.

It is worth keeping a light hold on the vision that God gives us. If you grip hold of the call for dear life, with the attitude that nothing is going to stop you from fulfilling this call, I would suggest that you may have a few character issues that may stop you from fulfilling the call and destiny of God. We all get it wrong. Perhaps you have got clarity on the vision but have added it up wrong. If you are travelling along using a compass and go one degree off course, it isn't long before you are totally in the wrong place. 'But it was only one degree!' Well, that is enough to be in totally the wrong place.

MAKE FAITH STEPS

However, with all the caveats out of the way, please don't let this stop you from making steps towards the vision that Father has placed in your heart. Take one step at a time, push some doors, have a go, and see what happens. Too much of the time the church is overly cautious about its approach to things, we are too fearful that something may go wrong – well, what if it goes right! I am the absolute opposite of risk adverse. I have always lived with risk and will always take risks. I can't see the point in playing it safe — that's not very exciting. Now I am certainly not expecting everyone to be as risky as me – you need to be true to the way God created you to be – but I do think that overall the church tries to be risk free. The journey of faith is full of risk and we need to embrace it. The clearer the picture that you are going for, the riskier you should be prepared to be —to the point where faith becomes so real that to step out in faith is no risk at all because faith has become so certain.

A true heavenly inspired passion will stick with you and develop as you commit yourself to God. Be inspired to give yourself to the call of God that will last your entire life, a call that will move you, motivate you, direct you, something that you will put your money into, spend your time on, get wrapped up in. We do this for jobs; we do this for some bizarre interests; let's be a people that get caught up with a heaven-birthed vision.

Three

OPEN HEAVEN

A few years back now, I had a brilliant idea that was going to turn the industry that I was involved in upside down. I remember having sleepless nights, not with worry but excitement, the sort of feeling that I remember getting on Christmas Eve as a kid, knowing that there were wonderful goodies waiting for me. This was the same. I had an anticipation inside that something great was going to break open with this amazing software/ internet product. The problem for me was not visualising the idea but communicating it to a target audience of software designers and marketers, but most importantly, financial investors! Getting across an idea simply and with enthusiasm in a few words is a skill that I needed to learn fast. Getting investment for a project running into a million pounds requires a certain skill —the ability to paint a picture of a vision that is workable and will succeed.

When God drops an idea into your heart you have a number of options. Sit on it for a few months/years to let it brew; immediately spring into action and get on with it; take time praying about it but never do anything. However, as you progress on a concept, as it is formed and takes shape, as you do something to visualise it, then the idea turns from being a pipe dream into a realistic proposition that could actually happen.

THE BUILDING PROJECT

A while back we started a major building project in the church. We have an impressive art deco cinema in all its 1930s splendour, but we wanted alterations to give us modern office space (rather than the shabby offices we had), a splendid meeting room, a high street reception, and modern book shop. I remember receiving the first plans back from the architect and getting the rush that comes when you visualise the reality of the idea. We knew in words what we wanted, but it was only when we saw it that it all began to make sense, the vision seemed like a reality. (Mind you, the reality struck home when I had to sign the contract!)

Getting a picture of the concept is crucial in taking vision from merely an idea to a workable plan of action. There is no real difference when you are dealing with dreams that God gives you. However, because we are dealing in 'heavenly' terminology and 'spiritual' matters we seem not to expect there to be any tangible, physical, visible sign of what it is we are going for. Why?

One of the reasons is because of the levels of our expectancy. We don't really expect any visibility to the vision. We seem to confine spirituality to some extra sense — something that isn't touch, feel, see, taste, smell. Why? Well I think it comes from our Christian tradition that mistrusts experience: 'Faith is what matters, and after all, faith is not seen, therefore anything which you may experience cannot be trusted because it is a physical, earthly sensation. We have graduated to a higher plane and don't need physical sensation to believe.' Ah, sorry! I think I would like a bit of experience to back up my faith. Well, let's explore what the Bible teaches about the role that our experience plays in faith.

STEPHEN SEES

"Look," he said, "I see heaven open and the Son of Man standing at the right hand of God" (Acts 7:56, NIV).

Stephen's is an amazing story of bravery, faith, encounter and, of course, martyrdom. The apostles were getting very bogged down with church admin — a problem common to many a church leader, even to this day. So they decided to get a few admin type people to join the team and sort out all the practical things so that they could give themselves to the word and prayer. Pretty legitimate as it is so easy to do emails and have endless meetings and not spend time seeking God!

So they chose seven guys to get on with the job.[1] Stephen was one, and this proved to be a pretty good strategy as the church grew as a result. Stephen was clearly a Spirit-filled mover/shaker. We assume he had the organisational skills, though nothing is said. But he had other qualities. He was filled with the Holy Spirit and moved in faith,[2] was full of grace, operated in power and was known for doing signs and wonders[3] —sounds like he should have led the church! He was clearly a persuasive sort of chap, presenting arguments about faith in a manner which just drew people, and had a depth of wisdom which was intoxicating. Now all this made him a pillar of the local church community and an easy choice for the apostles to hand over some responsibility to. But some got a bit hot under the collar with Stephen and started a vindictive campaign to get him discredited, ending up with Stephen being arrested and hauled up in court with trumped-up charges of blasphemy.

Well, I would have been anything less than gracious. I know how I am when I have to deal with some incompetent call centre, let alone being in this situation. But Stephen seemed to just shine . . . . Literally, his face *shone like an angel.*[4] He had grasped something, he had some inner peace and security. He was just not fazed by what was going on, almost as if he was somewhere else. Stephen's defence became a 'preach' on the history of the Jewish people,[5] which didn't do anything to endear him to the officials. It all culminated in the statement that *the Most High does not live in houses built by men*, which of course was interpreted as being blasphemous. They were similar to the very words of Jesus that caused him to be condemned to death. The court was *furious and gnashed their teeth*, but Stephen had his eyes fixed somewhere else . . . *he looked to heaven and saw the glory of God and Jesus standing at the right hand of God.*[6] Wow, what a sight! He was totally consumed with this experience of an open heaven right in front of him. It was almost as if he could reach out and touch what he was seeing; *'Look,'* he said, *'I can see heaven open, and there is the Son of Man.'* Stephen had this first-hand major experience of heaven; it was all real and alive to him at that moment.

What happened next was not at all pleasant, but it seems to fall away as being insignificant. The crowd jumped him and dragged him out of the city; he was stoned, but all the time we are left with the impression that the experience of what he saw eased him from this life to the next. Falling to his knees he prayed, *Lord receive my spirit. Do not hold this sin against them* (NIV), and, as if the day was over and it was time for night, he fell asleep!

Stephen saw something that amazed him, but I am convinced that what he saw was an extension of the life he was already living. He had such a grip on his heavenly destiny that no matter what happened he was going to tell it the way it was. He wasn't concerned with the court room, the allegations; he wasn't going to water down what he believed; he operated his life under an open heaven; he was a man who saw the supernatural as an everyday occurrence.

We live in an age when it is time for us as a people to operate under an open heaven. We should be a church of believers pursuing an open heaven agenda, living in the fullness of the supernatural overflow. Living on earth with the full force and power of this kingdom behind us. Scripture calls us to be ambassadors[7] and citizens of another place.[8] When the British embassy is set up in a part of the world it is like a mini Britain. The ambassador lives with the full power of his home country at his disposal, and that is what it is like for us as believers. Stephen grasped this reality, and although he lost his life, he had an experience of something else that far outweighed the life he lived. I think that is what Paul the apostle was getting at when he said, *to die is gain*.[9] Of course dying is gain when what you have experienced is so amazing.

JACOB'S DREAM

Jacob's dream at Bethel introduces us to this concept of open heaven, the gate and house of God. *He was afraid and said, "How to be feared and reverenced is this place! This is none other than the house of God, and this is the gateway to heaven!"* (Genesis 28:17, AMP). We see in this scripture heaven intersecting with the physical realm. In this instance Jacob has a dream where he sees heavenly pictures. Dreams seem to be one of the launching places for 'seeing' in the supernatural. Any regular bookshop will have several books on dreams. (I don't suggest you buy any!) The new age movement has tapped into a channel to get supernatural experience. Now don't get all spooked! God designed us to get access to heaven, and dreams are one of those ways. Just because dreams are a bit in vogue and have been hijacked by 'alternative' religion, doesn't make dream experience bad in itself. Come on believers, redeem your dream life for God. Ask God to speak to you in your dreams. I look into the biblical idea of dreams and visions in the next chapter.

F. B. Meyer says of this Bethel passage, 'There is an open way between heaven and earth for each of us . . . Jacob may have thought that God was local; now he found him to be omnipresent. Every lonely spot was his house, filled with angels.'[10]

JESUS SPEAKS ABOUT HEAVEN OPENING

Jesus speaks about the open heaven to his disciples, telling them that they will see it. *"I tell you* [plural] *the truth, you shall see heaven open, and the angels of God ascending and descending on the Son of Man"* (John 1:51, NIV). The way to heaven has been cleared; heaven is open; man may hear God and talk to him, as God had intended when he made man.

Jesus not only talked about open heaven, he also modelled it for us. He had a clear way to heavenly realities. Just look at his baptism. He was being obedient to the Father, modelling to us that baptism was critical, so he went and asked his cousin John to immerse him. Of course, John was hesitant to dunk his cousin in the water because he knew who he was! But Jesus insisted. *As soon as Jesus was baptised, he went up out of the water. At that moment heaven was opened, and he saw the Spirit of God descending like a dove and lighting on him* (Matthew 3:16, NIV).

What an amazing baptism service, one that we would all have loved to be at. The Father seems to pull back the heavens, like opening the curtains in the morning and peering out. The Gospel of Mark tells us that the heavens were torn. Father rips open the heavenly divide and speaks out how he feels towards the obedience of his Son. This is my loved Son, I am really chuffed with him. The Holy Spirit appeared in the form of a dove, which was reminiscent of the first time the heavens were open. The 'family' were at Jesus' baptism, and heaven and earth were connected.

To our secular, materialistic twenty-first century mind-sets, a visible spiritual event seems almost impossible. If it can't be proved by science then it can't really exist. So if you read this passage of Scripture with a mindset that needs logical scientific evidence you may well excuse it as merely a metaphor. I don't see this as a metaphor but as a real event. This was a moment of connection between heaven and earth where the reality of the heavenly realm was made visible in the physical, earthly realm. This was truly the kingdom of heaven at hand.

SIGNS OF AN OPEN HEAVEN

In the first eight chapters of Acts we see the birthing of the church, and in this time we see an open heaven. There seems to be a free flow of heaven onto earth, rather as it was around the birth of Christ, when a series of heavenly events burst onto the earthly scene – you may recall angelic appearances and the odd choir!

The other day I was on a trip and I was in my usual role of navigator. All the road maps that I ever buy always end up as loose-leaf, and I have to search through the detached pages in order to find the connecting page! However, as any self-respecting navigator will know, you need the road signs to verify your instructions. In the absence of signs you need some landmark to help you. The road sign confirms that you are heading the right way. Well, that is so true when it comes to what the Bible calls 'signs and wonders'. A sign points to something, directs you somewhere, a wonder leaves you 'wondering', in amazement and awe.

I believe that when God is around, when there is an open heaven, there will be a great many signs and we will be left in wonder at what we are seeing. Heaven is surely a place of wonder; you only have to read Revelation to get a glimpse of the awe that John felt in the presence of Almighty God. But in the early chapters of Acts we see a series of awesome events that point to evidence of an open heaven over the newly birthed church – something which surely should continue over the maturing church through the ages, rather than it going into decline.

'DECLARING THE WONDERS OF GOD'

I love the account of the Holy Spirit coming in Acts 2 — violent wind, fire on the heads of the believers, new languages bubbling up from the inside. The international assembly of Jews gathered in Jerusalem were able to hear the disciples declaring the wonders of God in their own languages.[11] The effect of a wonder, of course, is amazement and puzzlement.

In 1994, when many churches experienced a mighty outpouring of the Holy Spirit, people were left amazed and perplexed. Some, of course, spoke out and condemned that which they could not explain and justify from their theological understanding. Why are we so quick to justify and rationalise the wonder of heavenly experience? We write off anything that doesn't fit into our set of current experiences; we are sceptical of that which we can't actually explain very well. The rational, scientific approach has infused evangelical thought to the point where we forget that God is a God of wonder and mystery, and it is often through this wonder that he reveals himself.

After being well and truly dunked in the power of the Holy Spirit, Peter gets up quoting the prophet Joel. He prophesies the *wonders in the heavens above and signs on the earth below*.[12] The idea here is that the wonder of heaven is signposted on earth. The people were filled with awe,[13] and later with wonder at the healing of the beggar.[14] There is a pace in the opening chapters of Acts; they get this wonderful encounter of the Holy Spirit and it is as if all the lights come on and the disciples understand finally what Jesus had taken three years to teach them. The pages literally bulge with anticipation and expectation of signs and wonders; the wonder of the revelation of heaven seemed to be commonplace. I love that believer's prayer: *stretch out your hand to heal and perform miraculous signs and wonders through the name of your holy servant Jesus* – this is a time when the believers BELIEVED, a time when faith was heightened and the people were expectant of the miraculous.

So why is it that wonders are not a regular occurrence in the Western world? I have heard and seen much that convinces me of God's sovereignty and power in the third world, but have limited experience of the truly amazing, awesome acts in Western society. I firmly believe that it is, in part, to do with the hunger we exhibit for more of God. God has a habit of showing up when there are hungry people calling on him, eager to do what he wants them to do.

EXPECTANCY

The other dimension is a heightened expectancy of God to do something truly amazing. We have allowed the secular humanist mindset to infiltrate our thinking, to the point where we actually have bought into the lies that the secular modern world projects. Over years we have downplayed the wonder and the awe of God's supernatural world and settled for rational explanations, to the point where our default button is just accepting the rational explanation rather than the wondrous one. Twenty-first century sophisticated man needs to abandon the lie that has been bred in him that everything needs a rational answer.

The roots of scientific discovery were not initially a crusade to disprove God; rather, those scientists were on a voyage of discovery to understand the mystery of God. They had a hunger to discover more.

This idea of expectancy is also one which has been squeezed out of us by an increasingly cynical society which sets about pulling down everything that is achieved. The British must be the best at underestimating ourselves and defaulting to a cynical attitude. The American spirit, however, is much more expectant and entrepreneurial. (I hear my North American friends telling me I have too rosy a view of them!) We need to have an expectant spirit, one which is looking for the wonders from heaven. If you expect nothing then you will get what you expect! Now I am not advocating going around with an unreal attitude that sees a miracle in everything — please preserve us from getting into that mess! However, I do think we need to give up scepticism and sarcasm and take on a brighter outlook. Our expectancy goes hand in hand with what we see. I am advocating an active hunger for more of God's move, for God to reveal more of his design and mystery to us. I am seeking him, asking him, knocking down that door, wanting to get more than just a glimpse, but rather I want a good view of how God sees it.

I remember as a child trying desperately to find the Christmas presents that my parents had bought me. They, like every parent, had hidden them in a different place from the previous year; the excitement was unbearable. How anyone could resist the temptation of taking a peek to see what is going to be under the tree is beyond understanding. This is rather like the excitement and expectancy that I believe the Holy Spirit wants to kindle in us. He wants us to climb up to the top of the wardrobe, or look under the bed and see what is in store for us. Beloved of the living God, get hungry, get looking!

HEALINGS BECOME COMMONPLACE

The birth of the church age was accompanied not just by the wonder of tongues and a great sermon, but also by the miraculous, which just started to happen. Think of Peter as on his way to the prayer meeting and getting accosted by a 'Big Issue' seller who is obviously disabled.[15] Rather than just waving him off, or passing by without an acknowledgement he stops and speaks to him. The man, it says, was *expecting to get something from them* and he certainly got more than he expected! But note that there was an expectancy in the man. God doesn't seem to care if it was for something else — the Holy Spirit goes to work immediately in him. Peter's characteristic boldness, now refined by the Holy Spirit's power, kicks in and this man jumps up to his feet.

It is exciting that today all over the world there are accounts of healings taking place. There is a renewed belief that healings are not supposed to be the exception to the rule, but the rule itself. The Alpha course has helped enormously to build into the normal Christian's experience an expectation of healing. Preachers are tending to teach people to pray for the sick, rather than just the few travelling 'anointed ones' doing this. Now this rise of belief and expectancy is causing healings to happen. Because we are looking for healing, because we are seeking God for healing to happen —it does! This is a part of the open heaven—healings become commonplace; they were there in the everyday teaching of Jesus; they are there in the inaugural age of the church. We rationalised them away, but we are regaining ground. As a church we are not interested in healing happening just from the front of the meeting; we have people beavering away praying all the time, seeking healing as a normal experience. We have seen an increase in people's reports that they are healed. Some are difficult to document but others are dramatic.

Recently in Bath, two women who were wheelchair bound got up and walked! One lady who had disabling chronic fatigue heard someone say, 'Just reach out and take your healing,' so in simple obedience she did and was healed. She ran around the auditorium and amazed her husband when she arrived at the front door without the wheelchair. Another lady, who had only really known what it was to be ill, was 'soaked' in prayer, time and time again. She was faithful and gave thanks for every fresh indication of health, but she was still bound in her wheelchair. She kept on and on believing and not getting all resentful when her healing didn't seem to happen. Then one Sunday morning she came and stood at the front of the meeting worshipping – STOOD!

We are not flowing in anything like what we believe is the fullness of the healing anointing, but we press in.

We pray weekly for all those with long-term illness to see them released, believing that as we seek God and press in to him, we will see that open heaven. A while ago people were overheard talking on the bus about the healings that are taking place down at our church. That's the way it should be —the believers should be the talk of the town!

SALVATION, SALVATION, SALVATION

No matter how many times I read the book of Acts, I just can't get away from the fact that an open heaven means people give their lives to Jesus. It starts with three thousand, then *many believe*, then *numbers increased rapidly*;[16] this was a rapid church growth programme. I am getting desperate for more growth, real growth. I am blessed to lead a large thriving church, but if I am really honest the majority of the growth of the church has come from believers joining us from elsewhere. That is always going to happen, so I don't fight it, but I don't look for it. The real deal is conversions. The real sign of an open heaven is multiple conversions —people literally propelled into faith and the kingdom. I want to see authentic, life-changing, radical conversions. There is no point in getting converted on some half-truth and half-promise. I am not interested in increasing numbers on the basis of selling them a life-after-death insurance policy; no, we are called to 'make disciples', radical full-on believers with guts and passion. Bring it on, God! We want new birth. When new birth is turned on, church problems drop down the priority list; my needs become less important; the latest Christian fad doesn't seem all that important; we get a whole new set of priorities. Outreach has to be out of a passionate revelation of the Father's love for us! I am loved by the God of heaven, and that is available for every person on the face of the planet – any other motivation will end up with us just giving up. Give us the signs and wonders, give us the healings, but Father God, give us the lost.

Four

HEAVEN AT HAND

Ever forgot the key to the front door of your house and found yourself locked out? Well it's a pain, to say the least. You walk around the house looking for a window that is not shut properly, or hoping that the back door has been left unlocked, but of course it is the one day that you have been very thorough! It is quite a frustrating experience, 'This is my house and I need to be on the inside of it.' This is how we should be with the reality of heavenly experience. Our source, our vision, our dreams, our energy should all be on the inside of heaven, so if we are locked out no wonder we get frustrated and confused.

The dream that you are pursuing is either manufactured from a series of earthly wants and desires, or is put on the inside of you from the very throne of heaven. I believe that when you glimpse your destiny and identity from heaven's perspective then that vision will invigorate and sustain you. But it is getting into the place of heavenly experience that we need to have a look at.

After this I looked, and there before me was a door standing open in heaven. And the voice I had first heard speaking to me like a trumpet said, "Come up here, and I will show you what must take place after this" (Revelation 4:1, NIV). This is the starting verse for the general prophetic vision that John sees, which has become known as the Book of Revelation —probably one of the most misunderstood books of the Bible. John has just finished hearing the Son of Man dictate letters of instruction to seven angels over the seven churches of Asia Minor. Now for most of us, seeing Jesus and hearing him speak to us would be amazing, but to hear his instructions to the angels that are assigned to churches is mind-blowing. It doesn't stop there, now John gets an invitation to come up and get a heavenly perspective of future events —things that 'must take place'.

There is a similar opening at the start of the book of Ezekiel where the heavens were open to the prophet, and he saw visions of God. But in Revelation there is a door, which is 'standing open', with an invitation to come in. Here John is not stuck on the wrong side unable to get in, rather he is told to come on up. An open door is an invitation to come in. Just a few months ago I was decorating the hall stairs and landing – the most unenviable decorating job in anyone's house – and left the door open so all the dust would go out whilst I was sanding down the acres of woodwork in the hallway, and of course let fresh air in. One of my daughters comes home through the door and shouts, "Who left the door open?" And in my spirit I was reminded of the Revelation passage. Who indeed? In Revelation 4:1 why was the door left open and who opened it?

WHY IS THE DOOR OPEN?

In my decorating analogy I had a very functional reason for leaving the door open: to let the dust out and the fresh air in. When we are unloading the shopping from the car into our home, the door is open to allow a free flow of people and bags to make the journey from outdoors straight into the kitchen. When we are expecting lots of people to arrive at the house, the door is open so that they can just walk in. In the past we have had friendships with neighbours where they just walked into the house because we expected them to. Our family all have keys and can gain access whenever they want to.

The Revelation chapter 4 door is a powerful image of our ability to gain access to the Father in heaven. It is literally the doorway to heaven. The removal of the curtain in the physical temple was symbolic of the removal of any barrier between us and God. The way is made clear for us to gain access to God; our sin no longer separates us from him because the cross and resurrection have bridged the gap. Here we see that door – that way, that access point – in a real and powerful vision. This is the spiritual door that gives us entrance to the throne room of God. Don't let the word 'spiritual' be read as 'not real'. It is so easy to dismiss spiritual experiences as being in some way unreal, or subordinate to physical experiences. Our modernistic mindset that seeks to operate in the world of facts and tangible physical experience tends to naturally default to the wrong belief that if you can't see or touch it then it is not real. Christians have bought into this sensory life big time. We attempt to live by a 'spiritual' code, following the 'spiritual' directions of Jesus. However, we constantly try to ground all spiritual experiences into some greater earthly reality. I think that is why we get awed or sceptical when a notable physical healing takes place – it's this idea of proof. Healing sort of proves the reality of spiritual encounter. However, this is the wrong way round. In order to move in the supernatural – the miraculous – we first need to be reprogrammed as spiritual beings, walking in spiritual reality. If we do this then the natural signs and wonders will flow out of our spiritual reality. *And as you go, preach, saying, 'The kingdom of heaven is at hand'* (Matthew 10:7, NKJV).

JESUS' SCHOOL OF MINISTRY

Christ had this ease about his life. He was able to introduce people to the kingdom of God. The redemptive final act of death and resurrection was the end goal and object of his being sent to earth. There is no question about the purpose of God the Father sending his own Son; without that perfect sacrifice there was no hope for humanity's future. And Jesus spent three years proclaiming the concept of the kingdom of God (or heaven).

In Matthew's Gospel, Jesus gives instructions to the twelve disciples who were about to be sent out on mission. They were on an intensive Ministry School with Jesus and reached the practical two-week mission. What was their mission? Yes, to heal the sick, cleanse lepers, cast out demons, but that is the consequence of something else. Their project was to declare, *The kingdom of heaven is at hand*. John the Baptist introduced this theology,[1] calling on people to repent and declaring a new governmental dominion was here. Jesus picked up this exact same message; the first words of his ministry were, *"Repent for the kingdom of heaven is at hand,"*[2] and then the twelve keen students were tasked with the very same message.

Some versions translate this as '*near*', but it is more than near. The word suggests something imminent, a drawing near, and an active process of progressive closeness. Basically, the kingdom of heaven is not very far away; it is accessible and close by. If you think about the expression 'at hand', it really means it's here and available. I can lay my hand on it easily. Let's say you are sitting at your desk at work and someone asks you for some information. You may say, 'Hang on a minute, I can get that for you. It is at hand.' Now apply the same thinking to the kingdom of heaven. This kingdom that we are born again into and are a part of (in fact we then become citizens of it) is very near —so near that we can get our hands on it. We can access the provision and power of this kingdom easily. There is really a very thin layer separating us from the reality of the kingdom.

Many Christians have thought about the kingdom concept in two equally wrong ways. Either the kingdom is thought of as something that we only gain access to when we die, or the kingdom is confined to this world only. To me, the kingdom life that Jesus was talking about is a kingdom which he moved in and out of whilst he was on earth. He didn't just tell us about a kingdom of heaven (his home), he demonstrated easily the kingdom of heaven and how to gain access to it, and come from it.

The access to the miraculous lifestyle seemed effortless for Jesus. Remember the time when he had just completed the amazing feeding of the five thousand and then sent his disciples off ahead of him to prepare the next meeting![3] Well, Jesus went off alone to pray. He then clearly decided to meet up with the disciples, so obviously took the direct route – across the lake! He wasn't trying to catch up with the disciples who were in the boat struggling with the waves. He was about to pass by the disciples when they saw him on the lake. What follows is Peter's adventure on water. The point, though, is that Jesus was so engaged with heavenly reality that the idea of walking on water didn't faze him, it was no effort to do that. In fact, it was common sense because he just wanted to get to the other side of the lake.

'Come off it, Stewart, you are surely not suggesting that we all do that are you?' What I am trying to point out is that the access to heavenly reality is available to us, and if we can reformat our human hard drives and take on a new operating system we may just approach this life in a completely different manner.

That is why this Revelation 4 door is so tempting; it is calling us up to a higher place — a better place. This is not some metaphorical, allegorical door. No, I believe John saw his doorway to heaven. Sure, it was spiritual, but it was real. Behind this door was an alternative reality, one that could defy earthly laws, like walking on water, feeding five thousand with a few bread rolls, healing sickness – shall I go on? Hear the prophetic call. Father

God is calling us up, calling us to experience heaven now, calling us to operate from a different basis. That scripture that calls us 'citizens of heaven'[4] is absolutely on the button. Being born again gives us access to a whole different life, a whole new vista. Jesus is the gateway. But let's be very clear before I am accused of being a heretic: Jesus is the only means by which we access the Father in heaven.

Jesus said, *"I am the way, the truth, and the life. No one comes to the Father except through Me"* (John 14:6, NKJV). *For through Him* [Jesus] *we both have access by one Spirit to the Father* (Ephesians 2:18, NKJV). We have to go through Jesus, by the Holy Spirit, in order to gain access to the Father. Here we see that the Trinity is entrance, means and destination. We enter via Christ by the Spirit with the object of having a relationship with our heavenly Father.

However, Jesus goes on to say something further about himself. *"I am the door. If anyone enters by Me, he will be saved, and will go in and out and find pasture"* (John 10:9, NKJV). Here he introduces the concept of him being a doorway. Perhaps he is just using 'door' in a metaphorical sense to get across the idea that it is by him that we can get access to the Father. However it is a curious metaphor. Is Jesus the doorkeeper rather than the actual door? No! We have to go *through* the door to get into heaven; we have to go *through* Christ to get to the Father. This is one reason why, as believers, we need to be firm in our conviction that all roads certainly do not lead to God. No, there is only one way that people can go. Christ as the door makes a clear passage so that we can relate to the Father. If there is a message that is needed all around the world it is that there is a Father in heaven who wants to have a relationship with you.

However, look at the John chapter 10 scripture in a bit more depth. A door is in constant use and people come and go all the time. Since writing this chapter there have been six people using our front door. Doors are designed to enable us to go in and out. We are supposed to access the Father on a continual basis; there is this idea of being able to come in and out of the presence of the Father. Can you get your head around that? We are able to access the full reality of heaven on a regular basis, sort of like popping down to the shops to get milk! The milk analogy is useful because there is this idea of getting what we need from heaven for life —in this verse, *to find pasture*. We are being compared to sheep; we need to access the fullness of the heavenly resources so that we can have what we need. Jesus talks about storing up treasure in heaven.[5] This ease of access and getting provisions isn't to get by, eking out an existence, but rather we are supposed to have such a full life that it is described in verse 10 as *abundant*.

THE REALITY OF HEAVEN

Modern Christianity has done itself a massive disservice. We have tried to fall in line with secular thinking over the years and tried to rationalise our faith. Now don't get me wrong, thinking about stuff is really important, questioning, analysing all good. But modern Christianity seems to have diminished our immediate sense of heavenly reality. We go to church, say our prayers and read the Bible just in case it all proves to be true at the end of the day. After all, an eternity as the meat on a barbecue is no laughing matter. May I for a moment pose the idea that heavenly reality is more real than earthly reality. That spirituality has a greater eternal reality, much greater than our physical constraints— *. . we do not look at the things which are seen, but at the things which are not seen. For the things which are seen are temporary, but the things which are not seen are eternal* (2 Corinthians 4:18, NKJV).

Are we trying to see with our eyes or our spirits? The unseen spiritual things are eternal. Even faith is described not as a wishing, trusting faith but as a substantial, real, reliable faith.[6] Why don't we *set our minds on things above*?[7] It seems to be so hard, and we end up with a schizophrenic faith where our spiritual life amounts to an hour on a Sunday morning, which gives us a momentary escape from the monotony of 'normal' life! As we exercise faith we get to grips with the substance of heaven; by faith we gather evidence of eternal reality. *Moses kept right on going because he kept his eyes on the one who is invisible* (Hebrews 11:27 NLT). Rick Joyner has rightly pointed out that what we see with the eyes of our hearts can be more real to us than what we see with our physical eyes.

HOW IS THE DOOR OF HEAVEN OPENED?

When I was a boy scout I was taught by rote the Lord's Prayer. I suppose the years of saying what then seemed somewhat meaningless made this wonderful prayer and model of prayer dull and devoid of practical application.[8] However, closer inspection reveals great insights. As Christians we are talking to our *Father*, not a distant deity, but a loving Father. But look further: *Your kingdom come. Your will be done on earth as it is in heaven.* The prayer is all about seeing the reality of heaven manifest on earth. The prayer is a call to Daddy, 'Please Dad, come and help me here.' But there is more. Jesus goes on to describe the story of a friend and a neighbour.

I am just going around the house late at night doing the locking-up routine when the doorbell rings. There I am confronted with old college friends who have literally turned up at my door. Apparently they were on their way for a holiday and their car broke down. They knew that I lived near, so thought I wouldn't mind if they imposed. Of course not. "Come in!" Only trouble is they are starving and we have literally nothing in the house. My wife tells me to go next door to the neighbours and scrounge something —beans on toast will do! The problem is it's about 12.30 a.m., and my neighbours go to bed early. I ring their doorbell . . . the bedroom window opens . . . oh dear!

"What?" comes the voice. Well, I am very apologetic and explain the predicament. Effectively they tell me to go away as politely as they can. However, my wife's words are ringing in my ears so I press the point. In fact I press the point a little too much. I become, to my embarrassment, very pushy (not a quality normally associated with the British!) Now what does the character in the parable say at this point, and what is the application given by Jesus? *"Do not trouble me; the door is now shut, and my children are with me in bed; I cannot rise and give to you" . . . . I say to you, though he will not rise and give to him because he is his friend, yet because of his persistence he will rise and give him as many as he needs* (Luke 11:7–8, NKJV). The word here is persistence. The friend does not give in because he is my friend. No, it is because I am a pain in the neck!

The word 'persistence' means shameless insistence.[9]
The Greek here is *anaideia*, 'shamelessness', 'importunity',
'bold persistence'. Importunity means harassing with
persistent requests. Now remember the context of the
passage —it is all about prayer. Jesus tells this story to
help us to pray.

So how do we open up the door of heaven and keep
it open? How do we maintain that flow between heaven
and us? By shameless, bold and persistent requests to
God. This passage is not about the 'status' that we have
before the Father —Christians are his sons! This is about
continually accessing all that we need for life – abundant
life, getting what we need for the daily ins and outs. Come
on, believers! This is time to be bold, persistent, brazen
and outrageous in your requests of God. Literally you
should harass Father; not very reverent I know, but don't
blame me, look at what the Bible says!

I think Jesus was teaching us how to get the reality
of heaven; he was teaching us how to open up the door
of heaven. Remember the neighbour was locked in his
house – *the door is now shut* – so get it open. Do you
feel that heaven is all locked up and you can't access it?
Well get banging on that door! This is not a time to be
polite and reverent, this is a time to press in, persist!

Jesus continues, *"So I say to you, ask, and it will be
given to you; seek, and you will find; knock, and it will be
opened to you. For everyone who asks receives, and he*

who seeks finds, and to him who knocks it will be opened" (Luke 11:9–10, NKJV).

The key to the door opening is the persistent door knocking that we need to do. You want to receive the abundance that is there for you — well, get asking with bold persistence!

Five

KNOCKING ON
HEAVEN'S DOOR

The problem that most good evangelical believers face is the lack of 'reality' to our spiritual existence. We have so internalised our faith that spiritual reality is just locked up inside us. But actually our spiritual lives are bursting to get out and spill over into our physical worlds. This is why 'church' can be frankly boring and often will seem irrelevant to everyday life. To be honest, if Christianity only seems to have relevance on a Sunday morning then it is a complete waste of time. You may be forgiven for thinking: spiritual experiences are okay for you 'super Christians', but are not really for me. I entirely understand that sentiment. No, what I am driving at is that we have so diluted the 'experience' element of spirituality out of our lives, and made the Christian walk a rational journey, that we have completely lost the plot when it comes to the life-giving dynamic of living in the fullness of Christ.

This is a deep problem with the Western church. Christianity is often something we 'do', rather than it being the very essence of life pulsating through our veins. I have lived the majority of my Christian life trying to work out the reality of it all, and missing the point! We need to access the spiritual places, the heavenly courts, living as a son or daughter of God whose home is heaven. And this earth is a place of mission where we have been sent to make a difference. I want to be captured by a vision of something I haven't seen yet with my physical eyes, but have seen with my spiritual eyes. I want to be operating in a mandate given to me by the living God, something that I have experienced with my spirit. I want the friction of my spiritual existence rubbing against the physical circumstances, so that I learn to have supreme and total confidence in heaven when circumstances seem at odds with what I have tasted in the heavenly realms.

Don't think I am being all airy-fairy about this; anyone who knows me will tell you that I am very grounded and earthy when it comes to life! When I read the Bible I don't see elevated, superior people, I see the rough-and-ready earthy types who get God encounters, the reality of heaven bursting into their lives.

I love the way in which Jesus called that tough, manly man Peter, and turned him into the 'rock', a man in my reading of Scripture who couldn't be further away from Mr Religious, and gave him amazing encounters, teaching him to break into the heavenly realms and receive divine power for life. Then he took Paul, an incredibly religious person, decided that he was to be called for a purpose, impacted him while he was travelling, intersecting earthly time and space with an invasion of heaven, and made him into a most effective promoter of heavenly spiritual reality. You could be reading this and be a down-to-earth sort of person or a pious devout sort of person —this is for both and all in between!

LUKEWARM LAODICEANS

In the Book of Revelation there is a letter addressed to the angel of the church of Laodicea,[1] so instantly we should be sitting up and taking note, because this is a spiritual letter being sent to a spiritual being —the designated angel given responsibility for the physical church of Laodicea. What a great concept! Over churches around the world there are probably supervising angels with instructions from heaven for us. We are not here talking about colourful metaphors. No, we are talking about spiritual concepts that are real. A real letter to a real angel!

Now this isn't a great letter of encouragement — in fact it's a bit of a hard letter. The church has frankly become indifferent to God's word. They have just become like the community in which they live — nothing really distinctive about them, no real get up and go. Ever heard of that before? This is like the church in many parts of the West—indifferent, lukewarm, going through the motions of being a church. The message may sound to some ears pretty harsh at this point. They are certainly given a good old telling off, and are told in no uncertain terms to get zealous and repent of their indifference. The reward for shaking off the pathetic lifeless religion and overcoming is to sit with Jesus in heaven where he is enthroned.

In fact, my description above doesn't do justice to the language that God uses in the scripture. Here we have a completely complacent church that is so self-satisfied, has got itself in a rut, where the so-called spiritual life of the church is painful to watch, neither one thing or another, completely irrelevant! This church has grown fat, rich, in 'need of nothing'. You can get to the point that you don't need anything because you have made life satisfying. As I think about my own city, I fear for good people who live good lives, people who hold down jobs, pay their taxes, look after the kids, work hard, but have no spiritual understanding or desire. But the passage is directed to Christians who have become lukewarm, not unbelievers! As far as Jesus is concerned those he is addressing are wretched, miserable, poor, blind and naked, and the passage goes further, saying that they will literally be 'sicked up'. This respectable church is seen by God as fit to cause vomiting!

Now before you stop reading because you are utterly offended or feel hopelessly condemned, keep reading. *Behold, I stand at the door and knock. If anyone hears My voice and opens the door, I will come in to him and dine with him, and he with Me* (Revelation 3:20, NKJV).

We have a Father in heaven who has not given up with a church that is so repulsive to him. He is there for us, standing at the door knocking. It is not too late; we can buy gold from him that is purified, and white clothes so we will not be shamed,[2] and we can open the door to him and let him in.

Look at the order of things here. Remember we are talking of a church that has completely lost the plot, with no vision, no reality of heaven, no concept of the fullness of life the Father wants to lavish on his people. Whether you can hear him or not, he is standing at the door to you and your church knocking. You need to 'hear' him and then reply. Just a moment ago I heard our doorbell ring, but I didn't do anything about it (I seldom do!), but my wife went to the door and talked to the person, I heard them downstairs. You may well be in St Lukewarm Church, but the great news for you is that the living Lord Jesus is at the door, knocking on it. Just stop for a moment, hear him and let him in.

YOU NEED TO GET HUNGRY

But how? How do you move from the place of being consumed by this material world, locked into a consumerist view of humanity? You have got to get desperate! If you really want this heavenly reality then you have to get hungry and thirsty for it. Hunger is the only way to break the curse of being overfed. There is a demonic strategy at work in most of our lives in the West. It is called sensory overload. If humans can be kept busy, stimulated, visually satisfied, materially consumed, then there is no time or space for spiritual contact. It is a fact of life now to have constant music everywhere we go: in the car, walking along, doing your work – we seem to have a lust for noise at all times. The same is true with what we look at. Retailers stimulate our visual sense to make us buy, programme makers keep us engaged, advertisers entice us – today's world is full of of visual overload.

This sensory assault stops us from getting hungry; we are satisfied —well, sort of. Our material consumer lives dull the hunger, but never, of course, fully satisfy us. The need and quest for more stuff takes the edge off inner pain or hunger, but doesn't really deliver the real satisfaction. Retail therapy will never totally heal us. You have to stay on the retail programme for the rest of your life if you want to avoid dealing with the issues, and they still have a way of popping back up again unexpectedly.

The lack of spiritual hunger really is a twenty-first century problem. Retailers and manufacturers are getting wise to the need for spirituality, so they adopt an increasing number of 'religious' or spiritual logos and phrases to describe their products, as if this will satisfy the bit that is missing.

Now in case you feel I have totally missed the point, the Bible is pretty clear on the need to get hungry and thirsty. The psalmist cries out:

> *As the deer longs for streams of water,*
> *so I long for you, O God.*
> *I thirst for God, the living God.*
> *When can I go and stand before him?*
> *Day and night I have only tears for food,*
> *while my enemies continually taunt me, saying,*
> *"Where is this God of yours?"*
>
> Psalm 42:1–3, NLT

Isaiah asks "Is anyone thirsty?" The answer of course is, "Come and drink."[3] Jesus told us we would be blessed and filled if we were hungry and thirsty for righteousness,[4] and a little later described himself as the 'bread of heaven' —the right person to go to if you are hungry.[5] He used a meeting with a Samaritan woman to make the point about being filled very clearly. This lady was filling her buckets with water at the well. Jesus told her that naturally you need to keep drinking, but spiritually you can have an internal well bubbling up all the time.[6]

Stuck with a lukewarm life, you need to get thirsty. My own journey (and that of everyone I know who has got to the point of deep dissatisfaction) shows me you have to get very, very thirsty. I am now at the point in my journey of faith that lukewarm just will not do. I am not going to play at this Christian life any more. That means that I am going to break out of sameness and press on to get the job done, if it takes the rest of my life. I am not prepared to sit around and read a Bible that talks about the miraculous on the one hand but live a completely powerless life on the other. As I write this I cannot say that I move in miracles and see incredible healings all the time. I have seen some as I move out, and friends in my church family move in some as they move out, and I get reports of miracles and healings over the world as others move out. So perhaps my lack of testimony disqualifies me from telling you what to do. Perhaps, but I am on a journey where I have seen and experienced enough to determine in my heart that enough is enough; I want the full expression of faith in my life and not some part-payment! I am hungry enough – actually getting desperate enough – to go for this fully. No more living in Laodicea for me, no way!

Back to the Book of Revelation. Look what God will do if we open up the door. He will come in and eat with you. Not only will he come as you get hungry and desperate, but he will bring with him a picnic, which will satisfy you fully. When Jesus enters in fully, rivers of living water will brim and spill out of the depths of anyone who believes in him in this way.[7] So Jesus has definitely not given up with lukewarm believers – get hungry, guys! Do whatever it takes to get yourself into a place where God can come. Go where you can encounter him. Read stuff that draws you to him. Quieten your life to hear where he is knocking. My experience of getting hungry is that it is a process, and although there are many examples of dramatic encounter, in most cases he wants to woo you and draw you into a place of heavenly encounter over a period of time. The 'McDonaldisation' of life means that we expect what we ordered now, whereas my experience of God is that you will get it when it is the right time for you. You may have to wait years until you are really hungry —but you can get a real experience of a deep fountain. It is available.

PERSEVERING PHILADELPHIANS

The key to refreshing is perseverance. If you want to get this, actually experience the fullness of heavenly reality, get impacted with a vision that will last your life and be passed to the next generation, then you need to stick in there.

In the letter addressed to the angel of the church at Philadelphia,[8] there is no criticism because they had obeyed the command to persevere. They are encouraged to keep the faith, with the promise of a place in God's presence, a new name and the new Jerusalem. The persevering church comes in for no criticism; they are faithful and obedient, and stick in until the end. Many of you reading this should hear the delight of God in your lives. Some readers may begin to well up with tears because you know that God is speaking to you. You have had lots of opportunities to give up, many circumstances that seemed so overwhelming, lots of times when it all seemed too difficult. Sure, you have had moments of doubt, times of hopelessness, feelings of inadequacy, but you didn't give up. Well done!

In this letter, the one speaking has the key of David to open and shut whatever he pleases.[9] The key is, of course, authority, and Jesus clearly has the key of authority. But what has Jesus done with the keys that he has? *I will give you the keys of the kingdom of heaven; and whatever you bind (declare to be improper and unlawful) on earth must be what is already bound in heaven; and whatever you loose (declare lawful) on earth must be what is already loosed in heaven* (Matthew 16:19, AMP). 'You' refers to the disciples. So we, the 'inheritors', have been given keys to the kingdom of heaven. When we have a house guest we give them a key, so that they can let themselves in and out as they come and go. We have been given a set of keys to heaven. So we are able to see what is bound and loosed in heaven, and then bind or loose it on earth. We need to know what we have authority to do; we need to know our mandates. We need to look into heaven and see what is already bound in heaven and then bind it on earth. You need to get (spiritual) sight of what is bound and loosed in heaven, then do it on earth. So we know there is no sickness in heaven, it is completely bound there – so bind it on earth! We know there is no demonic oppression in heaven – so bind it on earth!

Look at these words to the Philadelphians: *I know your deeds. See, I have placed before you an open door that no one can shut. I know that you have little strength, yet you have kept my word and have not denied my name* (Revelation 3:8, NIV). Jesus is saying to the church that there is an open door in heaven for them, which is kept ajar for them because they have persevered. He has seen what the church has done and so has given them free and open access to heaven – you don't need keys when there is an open door in heaven.

This church had very little strength, but they stuck at it and didn't give up. That's great news for you who have persevered. Your steadfastness gives you an open door to the heavenly places.

HEAVENLY BLESSING

In the letter to the Ephesians, Paul writes that we have been blessed 'in the heavenly realms' with every spiritual blessing.[10] That means that we have massive resources available to us. What is the point in being blessed in the heavenlies unless we can get hold of blessings here and now? I don't mind the fact that they are spiritual because actually I am learning that spiritual reality is better for us than earthly reality. Surely my blessings are not supposed to be locked away in some vault in heaven until I die! No, they are there because moth and rust can't get at them,[11] and we are encouraged to actively put all the things we value in the heavenly account and not in an earthly bank. (I am not suggesting we are financial mavericks!) Heaven has an incredible deposit of blessing, stored up for us when we need it.

The LORD will open the heavens, the storehouse of his

bounty, to send rain on your land in season and to bless
all the work of your hands. You will lend to many nations
but will borrow from none (Deuteronomy 28:12, NIV).

In this passage, God gives Moses a bunch of promises.
He says that he will open the heavens (clearly a reference
to rain) to bless the farmers on the land. Here we see
God's desire to bless our work (physical) with rain from
heaven (spiritual). We don't have 'spiritual' stuff only,
one is supposed to affect the other! How do we qualify?
'Fully obey' the Lord and, 'follow all of his commandments'
(v. 1). Obedience and what we might call 'followership'
are the keys.

Most of the blessings in Deuteronomy are practical
and physical: good cattle, good crops, healthy offspring,
being blessed as you travel around, success in what you
do, visibly blessed in the nations, being at the top and
not the bottom — practical support birthed and supplied
from heavenly storehouses.

I think that the miracle of the manna given to the people
of Israel when they travelled in the desert is a brilliant
example of physical supply provided from heaven. God
literally 'gave a command to the skies above and opened
the doors of the heavens.'[12] What a picture! God's
starving people need food, God supplies it by opening
up the hatches of heaven and throwing it out!

The book of Malachi talks about abundance stored up.
It also talks about a purity and holiness, for the things of

God must return to the house of God before the 'day of the Lord'.[13] I love the last verse in Malachi that talks of the Father's heart and the children's response.[14] Christians have a great Dad who is looking and longing for his kids to return.

However, if we want blessing in every area of our lives we need to have an open heaven. I don't think that this just means financial blessing. Of course we want health, we want our families to be safe and successful, we want good relationships with one another, we want a deeper spiritual life. The Bible gives us a very clear idea of 'blessing' held in heaven and poured out upon us; the spiritual reality overflows to the physical domain.

Heaven is not just the spiritual end goal, it has to be consistently present and an immediate reality. We have to have the participation of heaven in our lives. If we don't, we are shutting out God.

HEAVENLY AUTHORITY

In his letter to the Ephesians, Paul compares the power we have on earth to the power that raised Jesus to his place in the heavenly realms.[15] In fact, we have been raised with Christ to be seated in 'heavenly realms' —it is our place.[16] When you go to the theatre you buy a seat for the show, then arrive at the theatre, present your numbered ticket and are shown to your seat. You are seated in the theatre, a place is reserved for you. Well, that is our status: a place in the heavenly realms. Sure, I may be operating for the time being on earth, but I have a reserved place. My name is written in heaven;[17] I even have a house all picked out and ready for me.[18]

God's intention is to reveal himself, to display his wisdom to the 'rulers and authorities in the heavenly realms'.[19] Great. How is he going to do that? Well, believe it or not, by the church! That means you and me as parts of the body working it out here on earth. So this church, which is on earth, is supposed to reveal the wisdom of God to the powers in the heavenly realms. Get the picture about how this church thing is supposed to work? We are parts of a body (Christ's body here on earth) that function together to reveal God around the world, but also to the heavenly realms. We are not supposed to live divided lives with earth and heaven as two completely separate realms, rather there is a flow from one to the other. Trouble is, we have so separated them out and made the spiritual one seem to some no better than a fairy story. I really believe many sincere Christians are living with a vague hope that this God and heaven stuff will come true at the end. 'Let's be believers just in case God is real after all, but please don't get too serious about it!' Can you see the lie and deception?

The apostle Paul goes on to tell us that we have a fight on our hands with the spiritual forces in the heavenly realms.[20] He clearly had a picture of a real spiritual battle, and we need real spiritual armour to get us through it. This is not just a metaphor, not just a pictorial illustration, there *is* a real battle. Come on guys, get real!

To me these passages just ooze reality, they bubble over with immediacy, they speak of something that we can't see, feel or touch with our physical senses, but which still exists. We negate spiritual realities at our peril. I feel there is something imminent in the prophetic voice; God is knocking, trying to awaken us from our materialistic, self-satisfied stupor. Oh, how stupid I have been to live out a conceptual Christian life, believing the theory but denying the experience! No more! I'll do what it takes to break what can sometimes seem like the 'silence' of heaven, by silencing my mind to the noise of earth.

Six

VISION INTO ACTION

Getting a vision and keeping it are two totally different things. I must admit to fluctuating between wild excitement at the scope of the dream that God has given me and feelings of total insecurity, thinking that all my noble plans are actually the result of a dodgy curry and too much beer the night before! Our dreams and passions can become sober when we face the routine of attempting to put them into action, so it helps of course when we can operate 'in faith' for our dream.

Now the second we start to talk about faith, believers conjure up a rather odd picture of what faith is. I think our sanitised version of Christianity has lost the dynamic of faith. We refer to 'our faith' almost as though it were like a lucky charm, or we talk about the 'Christian faith', faith being another word for religion or a collective noun. But what is it really?

I actually think the church doesn't really know what faith is! But without it you will never get your heavenly inspired vision to become reality. The writer of the letter to the Hebrews gets the faith debate off to a good start by declaring: *But we are not of those who shrink back and are destroyed, but of those who believe and are saved. Now faith is being sure of what we hope for and certain of what we do not see. This is what the ancients were commended for* (Hebrews 10:39–11:2, NIV, anglicised edition).

It is so easy to get a dream or a picture and 'shrink back', but then of course that is the plan of the enemy: get them to pull back from the seed of an idea that was planted in their minds. I love Paul's confident exhortation. We're not a bunch of woozies, no, we are pressing on! We need to get this confidence of faith, because without it we are going to fall at the first hurdle. Faith is the stuff that means that we will press on despite the circumstances that would scream 'give up'.

Hebrews 11 is a trip down memory lane. It is like looking at all those digital photos on your PC when you are a bit of a misery, recalling the good times. Well, these elders and ancients who went before us applied some key principles of faith which we would be well advised to follow.

Faith is the substance of things hoped for, the evidence of things not seen (Hebrews 11:1, NKJV).

We need to dig around a bit with two words —
'substance' and 'evidence'. Substance in this context
means 'something that lies underneath and supports
everything on top of it'. Rather like the specially designed
brickwork of a bridge which essentially supports the road
running across it.

Evidence is 'that by which a thing is proved and tested'.
For example, gold that is 'hallmarked' has been carefully
analysed and stamped to show it is what it is claimed to
be.

A dear friend and colleague of mine, Stephen Wood,
came up with a workable definition of faith: 'Faith is
the underlying rock-like structure that turns hope into
complete certainty, and gives concrete and irrefutable
proof that what we fail to see with our natural senses, is
in fact in existence.' I love it! Faith is not a wish, not a
'cross your fingers and hope that it will happen' faith, but
rather a rock-like certainty. The Amplified Bible describes
faith as the 'title deed', being convicted of the reality.
'Faith perceiving as real fact what is not revealed to the
senses' – yes, that's it, something of such certainty that it
is definitely there, yet our physical senses don't detect it.
So much of how we navigate our modern world is by our
physical senses. Being in a material world needs senses
to give us understanding. Everything we do in modern life
plays out in the physical world. Secularists would have us
believe that all that really matters in life is physical matter,

and spirituality is just a recreational pursuit, something that may bring personal benefit but should not be part of really important things. But faith is essentially something concrete, real, but not visible nor detectable by the tools that we use to understand the world around us. We need to learn to use our spiritual sense to see the invisible and hear the inaudible. Faith does not require us to use our natural senses; we enter the kingdom of God by faith. The whole point of this book is to explore the idea that we start from the basis of our spiritual sense rather than our physical sense. The reality and rock-like structure of faith is fundamentally spiritual.

God created the world, and we see in the opening chapters of the Bible how what he planned came to be. Hebrews 11 highlights the force of God's command in action—literally, physical matter comes into being by the word of God. The 'word' is spoken and the thing comes into being. God uses the word to bring matter into being. Just think on that for a little. God planned a planet teeming with life, and creatures who could have a relationship with him. We learn from John chapter 1 that there is even more to it than this, of course. There when it reads 'the word' (same English translation but different Greek word, *logos*) it refers to Jesus Christ, the second person of the Trinity, the person *by* whom everything was made.

God spoke. His word creates. Things happen. Matter

was created. For us, the creative process is different, of course. For a start, we are not creating something out of nothing! We are operating under him in the order he has created, whereas his creative act is sovereign and does not have any source outside himself.

But there are some points at which we can find analogies. God has made us to be creative, to receive our vision from him, to speak it out and act. We see that he encouraged Adam to be creative: naming other creatures, for example.

I have found (in recent years especially) that if you want to communicate a vision you have to find the right words to bring it about. You have to write down the vision and use words to communicate it to get people to buy into it and see it become a reality. Words carry a great deal of creative power. That vision, that dream, that idea on the inside of you can be spoken and commanded into reality. That can hold true in many areas of life.

Words from God are sometimes called (in NT Greek) '*rhema*' words. They can be very significant, building faith in us. God speaks to us, we hear what he is saying. That creates faith in us.

Romans 10:17 states that faith comes by hearing the word [*rhema*] of God. Faith comes by our hearing and responding to God's *rhema* (now) word, the word that he continues to speak today. A word of prophecy can be *rhema* (but do not forget that prophetic words must be tested in line with the biblical instructions); a word of knowledge can be *rhema*; the internal stirring and prompting of God may also be *rhema*. We sometimes call the whole Bible the 'word of God', as it is the authentic self-revelation of God's communication to us, against which everything else has to be checked and tested. Perhaps confusingly for new Christians, as we mentioned earlier, Jesus is also called (in English) the 'word' in John chapter 1 where the Greek word *logos* is being translated, which means, among other things 'creative principle'.

It is God's communication, his word spoken into our hearts, that produces faith — a concrete foundational structure that turns the things that we hope for into certain reality. We need to be quite sure that any word or vision we entertain is authentic — really from him. Faith in the word leads to the evidence. We are speaking of what is real, invisible and powerful. You can be motoring along and suddenly, pow, it hits you on the page! Suddenly the word hits you and you are aware it is living and vital.

So word produces faith — a concrete, foundational structure that turns the things that we hope for into certain reality. We realise that there is power in the word. We have to get to grips with spiritual realities that lie behind our physical world. So often we try to determine our spiritual world by what we can see with our physical eyes. We need God to speak to us (that might happen through our heavenly inspired vision perhaps); we need to receive what he says —let faith be generated on the inside of us, and let our actions and behaviour be in line with the spiritual certainties that we live by, which are to be in accord with his word.

When I was in business I had one of those life-changing ideas. I remember clearly lying in bed thinking about a software concept that I had. Every way I looked at it, I felt that it was a brilliant idea. This was a vision that stayed with me, consumed me, ate away at the inside of me. I believed it to be an inspired concept, birthed out of my relationship with God. By the way, God is very interested in the day-to-day routine of what we do. Part of the secular lie is that day-to-day work ideas have nothing to do with God. Nonsense! God is vitally interested in what we do between the hours of nine and five. So that means that God wants to give you solutions to problems that are pressing you, whether at work or home. I had to turn my vision into action, but I needed faith to be at work before I could step out in confidence. I had faith in this idea because I knew it was birthed in God, and I had a heavenly green light to go for what I was believing for. I had to stick my neck out, spend my money and allocate my resources to get this project off the ground. The result was eventually that the product got onto the open market and happened.

Now there is a set of principles here that can be summarised:

- *God speaks – a spiritual activity*
- *We receive – a spiritual activity*
- *Faith is generated – a spiritual activity*
- *Actions and behaviour follow – physical actions on our part.*

We will find it helpful to grasp these principles, if we are to run with the heavenly inspired vision.

SOME EXAMPLES

Next in Hebrews 11 we see a line of witnesses or testimonies to this actually working out in practice. It starts with Abel who got hooked onto the idea of offering God something that cost him something.[1] The first family were worshipping God, Abel offered the very best of his flock; he didn't hold anything back, he was open in every way to Jehovah. So what was wrong with Cain's fruit basket? Somewhere along the line, Abel heard the word that God deserved the very best of what we have, and this came out as an action. He brought a more acceptable offering by faith. This produced a righteous action. Abel understood the principle of holding nothing back from God – this word he heard created faith in him and he operated from the reality of hearing that word. This act of sacrifice cost him his life; the evil desire on the inside of Cain ended in Abel's death.

Next up was Enoch,[2] a man who 'walked in close fellowship with God'. He and God were buddies. Then, one day, Enoch disappeared. No body, no funeral, he just went! The closeness with Father was such that the physical disappeared into the spiritual; the spiritual in this instance was a far greater reality. The only way to please God is by faith.[3] Enoch's righteousness was such only because faith was allowed to percolate through him.

Noah also 'walked in close fellowship with God',[4] so God's word was flowing between him and God. The world had become so bad that God was pretty sorry that he had ever started the 'mankind project'. He was ready to start all over again, press the reset button, and Noah was his new Adam. God spoke, faith was created, and Noah acted on faith. It wasn't the fact that Noah did good things that made him righteous, it was the fact that he allowed faith to develop and blossom in his life.

Noah was 'crazy' enough to do the impossible. He started to build the biggest man-made structure ever made —because God spoke to him! Was this some madman who did the ridiculous? He didn't know he was not supposed to build an ark. Noah had no more access to God than you and me, yet we suppress the call of a 'crazy' life to live a sanitised version of what God intended. Noah 'condemns' mankind by his faithful actions . . . . He chose to believe what God had told him rather than what was all around. So finally it rains and he is saved, on board the first cruise ship for a year! Noah's actions were generated by faith; these actions had enormous consequence for the human race.

Has your vision ebbed away from you? Have you allowed the still, small voice of God to drift away into a dim memory? Because you did not respond to the divine idea, have you let go of something which would have become your destiny? Without the ark, Noah would probably not have even made it onto the pages of Scripture. Can you imagine if Noah had not listened to God? Can you imagine if Noah had written down what God had said —and had then slowly just forgotten about it, letting the heavenly vision get diluted by business and circumstance? Ridiculous, isn't it? But that's what happens to us so often. God gives you a dream, a desire, an idea; he presents you with a destiny, and it's up to you to respond to it.

These characters in Hebrews all illustrate this point, responding to the word that comes from God, no matter how difficult and impossible. Abraham got spoken to by God[5] —to move on from the land of his fathers called Haran, and go to a place he didn't know, a land that God would show him. Now his dad, Terah, had originally set out from Ur — down the motorway to Canaan; but on the way they had stopped off at Haran service station —

probably for a cappuccino and croissant. However, Terah, in his wisdom, decided to stay there. So when the call came from God to Abraham to go, God decided to speak to the sons rather than the fathers —they had had their moment. Vision, I believe, is deposited with individuals, but if they do not respond, if they get sidetracked, if they simply don't want to do whatever is called for, God will find someone else to do it. He is very patient about waiting for us to respond, but when he wants it done he will get the job done. Perhaps somewhere along the line you got stuck at Haran and compromised the call of God? However, here we see it again: faith bringing about action. Abraham heard what God said and went. It wasn't all that clear; he couldn't speak the language; he was going to be the stranger, but it was time to respond to the word. (More on this story in chapter 8.)

A picture of a heavenly home was imprinted on Abraham's heart.[6] He was captured by a heavenly image of a 'design and build' city. Gripped by something that had its origin and completion in God, and yet he was being asked by God to be a part of it. Here is faith at its best – God speaks the word, the word takes root, faith is established. That became the bedrock of Abraham's life.

To top it all, Abraham and Sarah couldn't have kids. This was a disaster because they would have been stigmatised, and it made them pretty miserable. Not to be personally fruitful must have felt like God had totally abandoned them. But Abraham just couldn't get away from the fact that God made this promise to him that he would have a son. He makes the promise several times in Genesis chapters 15 onwards, creating a picture of a great nation and descendants as numerous as the stars.

Even Abraham became completely incredulous about God's insistence, "I'm over one hundred years old." Was he tempted to think the voice of the Lord was just his colourful imagination? No, Abraham's action showed that he believed in it and 'it was credited to him as righteousness.'[7] Abraham and his wife, Sarah, even tried to help God along by getting Abraham to have sex with the cleaning lady. It seemed to them quite a sensible arrangement that could fulfil what God had said.

When God says something, it is going to happen. It may not happen in your timing, in your plan, in a way that even fits in with you, but it will happen.

How many of us hang on to a vision we feel is inspired by God, then downgrade it to a good idea, then to a 'one day I hope', to a 'I used to think that', to a memory that can't possibly come about? Come on, family of faith, it's time to take God at his word and stick with what he has promised. However ridiculous and impossible it may seem, that's what faith is all about. In the midst of the ridicule, when it makes little sense, when it is inconvenient, when it costs your dignity, when you are in the darkest place, that's when you need to rely on the firm structure of faith.

How cavalier we are sometimes with the word of God. How disposable and instant we seem to think the word of God is. Do we treasure and store up the word of God? Do we allow it to take root and bear fruit in our hearts?

My business life went through great times and then a very bad patch. However, in the midst of raising venture capital funding, with all the excitement of huge potential in growth, God spoke to me about being on a training course lasting three years. I didn't really understand what that meant. I was up to my eyes in business plans, but I just held on to this word. I was pretty sure that it didn't mean that I should go on a course, but that the next three years would *be* a course. Well, over that time I was able to raise a million pounds in venture capital funding, have some early big successes, then see the market change before my eyes, and the possibility of making money seemed to vanish. Eventually the business went into liquidation and my once admirable business character and all my pride went completely out of the window.

Sitting in my office, which was now my front room at home, scratching about to make a living, I was reminded that my three year training course was coming to an end.

Then, as if out of nowhere, circumstances changed

in the church that I had been part of for fifteen years and I found myself on the full time leadership team. Ah, I get it now! All my experience of the 'big time' was a preparation for me to pursue a different aspect of building the kingdom, through the church.

BEING PRACTICAL

It is worth focusing on what it means to bring about your dream into a reality. How do you actually do it? Well first of all we need to remind ourselves of the principles that we identified in this section.
1. God speaks – a spiritual activity
2. We receive – a spiritual activity
3. Faith is generated – a spiritual activity
4. Actions and behaviour follow – physical actions on our part

GOD SPEAKS

There is no point in pushing out on something that will demand your life and energy unless God has spoken to you. In chapter 7 we will look at this in more detail. Hearing God's voice should be a normal Christian experience, not something that we constantly doubt. We need to get a conviction that God has spoken into our spirits about the project or plan. This is the fundamental difference between having a good idea and having a plan that is of God. Cultivate the conversation between you and God. When we develop that flow of communication, it's amazing the things that God is actually saying; the ideas we have will be birthed out of this conversation.

WE RECEIVE

Cleaning out our spiritual ears is well overdue for the church. We can sometimes be good at speaking, but have we cultivated listening to God? The charismatic church has emphasised vibrant worship, but what about hearing the voice that comes in silent contemplation? As usual the church throws the baby out with the bathwater —we need both. But bringing about your plan is more than just hearing, it is about letting the word take root. Like planting a seed in the soil, something mysterious happens to the seed in order for it to start its work. The seed takes root in the warm soil in which it is planted, it is received by the soil and something happens. If you have a dream, you need to prepare and cultivate the soil of your heart —or otherwise that seed of faith will never actually get started.

FAITH GENERATED

Taking the seed analogy a little further, faith will start to emerge just as the seed breaks into a plant. You may not see any evidence of this as it is tucked away under the soil, but in the dark, faith like the seed is growing. This is key in the process of 'vision to reality'. You have a word that has come from Father, you have prepared and cultivated the soil of your heart to receive the word. Now faith can be generated. And you act on the word of God.

ACTIONS AND BEHAVIOUR FOLLOW

Once this faith project is beginning to get a grip on you, you will change your behaviour in line with the word of faith in you. When I hear of what God wants to do with me, or with the people I am working with, my behaviour comes in line —to play my part. That means that I think differently, have a different set of priorities, organise my finances differently, make different decisions – all based on the faith that I have for the vision.

As a church we have heard God tell us to be a resource to other churches. This is not out of boasting or a sense of superiority. No! Rather, it is birthed out of the word that has come to many people and has generated a sense of conviction that this is what God has called us to. For many years we were not really living in line with the word that had come, so we started to change our corporate behaviour to be in tune with what God would have us do. This has meant ploughing considerable resources into conferences, our magazine, and making the preached word available. Some cynics will say we are just becoming commercial, but the reality is that we do this because of a *faith response* to the word of God.

So many believers hear a word, cultivate themselves to receive the word and have faith, but then do nothing to actually bring it about. We have to change our mindsets and our actions to come in line with what we are pursuing. Most secular books that talk about this subject of vision to reality will emphasise this point, and then give lots of practical tools to help you achieve that shift. There can sometimes be value in such approaches in certain contexts, but the starting point for the people of faith has got to be the dialogue with God – get it from heaven first! For a Christian, real 'positive thinking' must start with God's voice.

Living the vision means living by faith. God is always speaking to us—we have often just got too much spiritual wax in our spiritual ears to hear him. We need to receive what he is saying, hear it and take it in. You don't have to make it up, you don't have to pretend; but, when he speaks, do some listening. If you have never had a prophetic word or never really sensed him speaking to you, read the written word that he has given us – the Bible – and just start to hear him! Remember to pray for the Holy Spirit to help you to hear his voice speaking to you as you read your Bible. You will find that something amazing happens: faith is generated on the inside of us. This is a rock-like structure. Then we start acting in line with our faith, no matter what the circumstances around us, no matter how daft it makes you look — that's the adventure that we have been called to.

Seven

KNOWING GOD'S VOICE

To pursue a vision birthed in heaven we have to get an understanding of heavenly reality. In order to make that dream a reality, we need to learn the ways of faith. In order to get faith we need a word from God. In order to get a word from God, we need to hear what he is saying.

Jesus described himself as the 'good shepherd'.[1] He is the one who legitimately enters the sheep pen, calls the sheep out, and all the sheep follow the voice of the shepherd. The sheep sense that the shepherd only has their very best interests at heart. He is not going to deceive them, he is not going to lead them into danger; on the contrary, he will lead them to a safe place. Great illustration, even if you don't have an agricultural background; it illustrates dependency, trust and a need to follow.

Many contemporary Christians seem to find it extremely hard to listen to the voice of God. Jesus knew how to hear the Father's voice, but we find it so hard to tune in. Somehow, modern believers seem to live on very dodgy ground when it comes to what they believe. It is more often a 'blind faith' rather than a faith based on a real relationship. The number of Christians who cannot actually tell you what God is saying to them is staggering. It has become normal to be uncertain and unclear. How many times have you heard people say, 'I don't know what God is saying'? What has happened to us to remove our certainty of hearing God? When I read the Bible, I see that most of the characters didn't seem to have trouble hearing God. It seems to report God speaking very clearly, and I am pretty sure his voice wasn't physically audible all the time (although of course God does speak audibly sometimes).

I wonder if by reducing God to a 'personal saviour', by compressing our experience of him to the realm of the known – the sphere that can only be experienced by our physical senses – we have made the mistake of restricting our understanding of the voice of the Creator God to the constraints of the created world. If you discount the 'supernatural' experience, treating it as being like a fairy story, you limit the way in which you are able to hear God speak to you. Your attitude becomes: 'It is okay to have it in the Bible, but it doesn't happen today' – or, 'If it does happen today it doesn't happen to people like me, it only happens to a spiritual elite.'

So what happens is that we confine our experience of hearing God to reading the Bible, having a 'feeling' about something, a hunch; interpreting circumstances, and taking good advice from trusted elders of the church. Now before you chuck this book away as being complete heresy, I am not saying that any of the methods I have mentioned should be discounted. The Bible is, of course, the authentic and living word of God, full of spiritual life for every situation we could possibly face. Our feelings and circumstances are not desperately reliable on their own (indeed they may seem to run counter to the truth God has placed in our hearts, feelings may be deceptive, circumstances may be testing, and there may be battles to be fought there), but linked with other ways of hearing God, they can have validity. And, of course, take wise and godly counsel and be prepared to hear and weigh words of confirmation or warning. There are, then, tangible, sensory ways in which we can discern the voice of God. But hang on a minute! We have lost a whole load of other ways in which God speaks to us, ways that are entirely spiritual. Remember that you have a spirit, and God is Spirit, so he can communicate with you, a Spirit-filled believer, at a spiritual level. You can hear him inwardly in your spirit.

SPIRITUAL HEARING

'Feelings' are a fragile commodity. The 'I feel' statement gets something near to sensing God with non-physical senses. It is commonly held that humanity is made up of body, soul and spirit, and it is the 'soul part' where feelings are to be found. Many argue that soul and spirit are interchangeable in Scripture, and that the differences are not biblically clear, although it would be true to say that the basic Hebrew view of a person stresses their unity rather than these distinctions. Well, don't get hung up on the theology of this, but rather see that the idea of 'feelings with which we sense something' gets us close to understanding 'spiritual hearing'. Now, if it weren't for the fact that our feelings can be incredibly unreliable they would be very helpful in the process of tuning in to God. Why are they often rather unreliable? Because of the years of emotional wear and tear that they are put through, not to mention the fact that they sometimes reflect something of the old nature against which we all struggle, even after we become a new creation at our new birth. Now I know that I have lost you if you are an analytical, logical type of person, someone who likes to gather facts and data. But even the most Spock-like human can't completely disregard the powerful hold that emotions have over us. Perhaps we have discounted feelings as a way of hearing the voice of God because of the fragility of emotions, but I think you may be forgetting that God actually seems to prize weak and fragile people. In fact, he seems to demand that the strong become weak, because it is only out of weakness that we really understand true spiritual strength.[4]

Many Christians have bought into the material world-view big time. In order to connect with a culture of modernity, we have learnt to rationalise the gospel, explain the text, have an apologetic, and formulate an argument. Rising secularism demands that if the world is going to take faith seriously, then you need to prove it. We have made a science out of faith. I have hundreds of books in my study all helping me to 'prove' my faith. We have, frankly, lost the plot. Why has the battleground shifted to science, logic and being rational, when Scripture clearly shows us that the battle we fight is not human, material or physical?[5] Yet we make our battle earthbound when we should be participating in the heavenly victory. The atheistic secular rationalists will never be defeated by wise and persuasive words; the spirit behind them will be defeated when we participate as co-heirs with Christ, the victor!

The church in our recent history seems to have its sights set extremely low. It is almost as if we have accepted the fact that we are a remnant, and these are the last few days of a closing-down sale before everything must go. Well, that is just not the case.

When we start to get a supernatural or heavenly view, things happen a bit differently from what we are used to. In fact, we will soon begin to expect our communication with heaven to be a little odd, or even bizarre. I have a sense that Father God is keeping us on our toes and making us operate in the faith realm.

Mark Virkler has some great teaching on hearing God's voice. He uses the language of tuning into the Spirit with a 'spontaneous flow' of his word to us. Focussing on the person of Christ, we begin to get a bubbling up of the 'now' word of God to us. I have many moments when this happens. I am privileged to live on a hill overlooking my home city, and I will often 'self-talk' as I walk up the hill. Now, I may seem odd to passers-by, although I will often put my mobile phone to my ear to pretend I am on the phone, so it doesn't seem so weird! As I mutter and talk to myself, there is a bubbling up on the inside and I start to speak out God's word to myself. It amazes me the things that come out, things that I would never have thought of, things that correct me. I have learnt over the years to allow that bubbling up to come out of my hands and onto the page in front of me. I have many pages of text that just erupt from my fingers on the keyboard, which when I review with my head afterwards, make fascinating reading.

Before I just highlight some of God's communication methods that are being seen again in the church today, I want to be clear about the role of the Bible in hearing God's voice. Many excellent books will prove and validate the inerrant, infallible living word of God that we call the Bible. Be under no illusion reader, if you don't read the Scripture then no other method of hearing God's voice will be of much value. Scripture is the measuring rod for theology, doctrine and erroneous thinking. It is the metronome of our faith, the timeless jumping-off point for a God encounter. Is God interested in experience and feelings? Of course. But if you let Scripture grip you, your desire for the depths of Father will increase. It is worth saying that in all the renewal circles that I am involved in, which may emphasise feelings and experience, what I notice is an increased passion and hunger for the written word of God. You can't really go deeper with God without the Bible figuring as your top priority – be warned!

PROPHECY

My experience of the gift of prophecy in action is that you have to learn to 'tune in to' the Holy Spirit. From our perspective it can seem spontaneous, but when it is authentic (and the Bible gives us criteria for testing it), it is a way God speaks. Prophecy comes like a bubbling up, and you speak what you hear. Sometimes it starts with a picture, sometimes with an affirmation, but there is certainly a flow. I have seen the prophetic ministry amongst ordinary people increase in effectiveness over recent years. As a local church we have set ourselves to press in to God for more of the flow of his prophetic word, and have sought to release a pure quality of inspired words.

At our church we have a team who speak prophetic encouragement over people before the Sunday meeting. Visitors will ring in beforehand and book an appointment. Three or four members of the team will then ask God to give them words for the person, and then they go around in turns and communicate what God has given them. We record it all on a tape and give it to the person. It never fails to impress me as to the degree of accuracy that comes. Ordinary Christians, who have decided to pursue a gift that is not easily understood with the mind, are able to encourage the person, know things that they wouldn't naturally know, and build someone up. To see people helped by personal prophecy is wonderful. God uses weak and fragile people to communicate his lavish plan and love for someone else.

Now, I am not naïve enough to think that it never goes wrong, and that we never get it wrong. We prophesy in part;[6] and we only see a poor reflection;[7] and I am not pretending that my spontaneous writings are always the exact word from God, nor somehow on a par with Scripture! However, as we are refined and sanctified, God seems to do some unblocking in us, one effect of which is to open us up to hearing him more readily. We endeavour to get, as one of my prophetic friends would say, 'a purer stream'. We are working on this at the moment in our church. How do we take the pictures of battleships, soaring eagles and trumpet blowing angels on the hills, and translate that into what Father God is saying to us right now?

A while ago I was in Uganda, visiting some dear friends. It was the same time as the World Cup, and because England was playing we were all sitting outside as the sun set with about twenty of us watching a small TV. Our African hosts spent most of the match trying to get a good signal. The best signal was on top of the tin roof of the accommodation block. So here is the scene. One of the Ugandan brothers, hanging onto the aerial, pointing it to the stars, with all the English fans shouting, 'A bit more to the left'! Well that is so often our approach to the prophetic. We are waving our aerials, trying to get a pure signal. When I bought our digital TV receiver I plugged it in and there it was, a pure signal. God is emitting a pure signal, but we seem to be struggling with an old aerial. However, there is a pure stream of undiluted gold coming to the people that will seek him and call on him.

DREAMS

If you go to any bookshop you could easily buy a book on dream interpretation (I don't recommend this by the way). Why? Because people are searching for ways to uncover direction in their life, when the rational, logical approach of our society is failing. So there is a boom in interest in dreams as a way of understanding our futures and ourselves. There is much deception around in such secular literature, but even the most cursory study of Scripture will shine up the fact that God has used dreams to speak to his people as a normal way of communicating with them.

Dreams are often symbolic and figurative, and most of the time do not mean exactly what you see. An obvious example is Pharaoh's dreams[8] of seven scrawny, emaciated cows eating seven fat, beefy cows, and the thin, shrivelled grain heads swallowing up the bulbous, plump grain heads. Now this was not of course literal, but the dream was infused with meaning and needed Joseph, a gifted dream interpreter, to apply the dreams correctly. Clearly, God was interested in communicating something to the ruler of the most powerful nation on the face of the known world. He was interested in forewarning them about a disaster that was seven years away, but if action was taken their prudent short-term decisions would affect the long-term future for the nation!

Dreams have many and varied purposes. Abimelech rather took a fancy to Abraham's wife, Sarah, after he was led to believe she was Abraham's sister. He was going to 'sleep with her' and God warned him in a dream not to commit an unwitting sin.[9] So this sort of dream gave him a piece of knowledge which prevented him from committing a sin which would have brought him under God's judgement.

Daniel faced a similar situation to Joseph.[10] He is a young apprentice diplomat in the royal university who suddenly finds that he and and his three flatmates are facing a death threat because none of the supposed wise men of the court can interpret the dream of the dictator king, Nebuchadnezzar. I can just hear the king shouting, 'What do I pay these fools for? Kill the lot of them.' Daniel, being the sweet talker that he was, managed to buy a bit of time to get on his knees in desperate prayer. He then had to tell the ruler the dream and interpret it for him. God shows up —phew! And he gives Daniel the secret that he needed. Emboldened by the fact that God spoke to him, Daniel's faith begins to operate, he saves the day, and gets promotion in the court.

A few chapters later, the king has a follow-up dream, which Daniel is more than a little bit nervous about interpreting because of the potential consequences. These are significant dreams with significant consequences. The dream had a massive effect on the life of the country, and both Joseph's and Daniel's ability to get answers not only influenced the course of the nation, but also elevated them to positions of influence. Of course, in the West the idea of nations being turned from disaster because of a dream seems ridiculous to our secular mindset. But why? Do our rulers not have dreams? If they do I am sure that the sceptical media would laugh off the idea that God could warn the Prime Minister of the UK or the President of the USA in a dream!

At Jesus' trial, Pilate was sitting in judgement over Jesus, having a hard time coming to a verdict about what to do with him. Free him or crucify him? Pilate's wife has a terrible nightmare about Jesus' innocence.[11] Consequently Pilate really fudges the issue and refuses to take responsibility for what the crowd wants to do. Dreams can give us unique knowledge and discernment about a course of action that we are considering.

Jacob has his famous ladder dream at Bethel,[12] where he exclaims that this is the house of God and the gate of heaven. God makes a staggering commitment to Jacob (who looks to me at this point like a bit of a rogue) by giving him the land upon which he is sleeping and telling him that his descendants will spread out and occupy it. Jacob rubs the sleep from his eyes, clearly reeling from a sense of impending destiny on his life, and sets up something to remember this astonishing moment by creating the first sculpture park!

Dreams can launch a person's destiny. Joseph[13] may have been naïve, brash and foolish when he declared to his ten older brothers that they would all bow down to him, and even his doting father got a bit shirty with him when Joseph suggested that his mother and father would also bow down. You would have thought that Joseph really would have kept his dreams to himself. But his dreams came true, although he had to endure considerable sacrifice and hardship first! Perhaps there is a warning attached to dreams of destiny: don't be too quick to talk about them to others, and take your time, because with the destiny will come responsibility and a whole load of character building!

God warned Laban in a dream,[14] the wise men altered their travel plans by a dream,[15] and Joseph moved house, job and town with Mary and Jesus because of a dream.[16]

My wife and I made a life-changing decision on the basis of a dream that I had. We were in our twenties, relatively newly married, and God spoke to me in a dream about moving to Bath to live. Deborah confirmed this when I told her in the morning by saying, "That's interesting, God has been talking to me about that for the last few months" —which of course I knew nothing about! Now being young and simple, we took my dream as a confirmation. Why wouldn't God speak to me in a dream? I think it is the last twenty years that taught me to be sceptical about making a massive life decision on the back of a dream – and that is what I am having to unlearn.

I am really quite taken with this idea that dreams can provoke an action, that we are given a dream not only to alert us, or to foretell, but also to lead us to do something about it. Gideon was a pretty impressive general. God tells him to take his army of thirty-two thousand and take on the might of the Midianite alliance that had amassed on their borders.[17] This was going to be a brutal battle. However, as is so often the case with Jehovah, if it makes sense with natural eyes then it probably is not a faith exercise. Gideon follows God's instructions by reducing the size of the army from thirty-two thousand to ten thousand, then to three hundred – eek! Not surprisingly Gideon was a little nervous about the battle.

When God tells him to sneak down to the enemy camp, there were soldiers absolutely everywhere. He would need more than the massive army he had told to go home, let alone a ridiculous three hundred who were selected not because they were hardened marines but because they drank water with their hands – not the best recruiting methodology for an army! In the shadows he overhears words that engage his soul and galvanise him in faith to fight the battle. He heard an unnamed man in the camp talking innocently about a dream to a mate, and its interpretation galvanised Gideon to believe that with three hundred hand-drinking soldiers he could defeat the Midianite hordes! A dream and interpretation caused an action, which brought incredible victory!

What is our problem? Have dreams been captured by new age thinkers so that they can't be a serious modern way for God to speak to his people? Will it make us look silly and ridiculous to trust dreams? Joseph decided to wed Mary because an angel spoke to him in a dream,[18] and Jesus claimed his Jewish lineage via Joseph's ancestors.

In the Old Testament, dreams were a normal way that God spoke to his prophets.[19] However, when the Holy Spirit comes upon the early church, Peter quotes the prophet Joel,[20] and everyone gets the opportunity to receive the Holy Spirit – not just the prophets – and the tools of the prophetic trade (namely visions and dreams) are given to young and old men. Maybe one reason older men need to have a Sunday afternoon nap is because 'old men will dream dreams', and after all, you can't hear God in a dream unless you are asleep!

In considering your destiny, your future, your potential, your heavenly inspired vision, consider King Solomon. He had an incredibly hard act to follow. His father, King David, left him with a mandate to build a temple for Jehovah. Solomon was a man with destiny hanging over his head. But one night the Lord chose to appear to Solomon in a dream to ask him to choose whatever he wanted.[21] He didn't choose riches and fame, but wisdom —the quality that every leader will need if they are to accomplish their life vision. God, being pleased with Solomon's decision, chose to give him a depth of spiritual wisdom as well as riches and fame! Then Solomon woke up. Now if a physical dream is a way in which God chooses to communicate with his people, then God, please talk to me in dreams. If dreams challenge, warn and foretell, then I want more dreams. If angels, and God himself, appear in dreams, then Father can we meet sometime between 11 p.m. and 7 a.m. any day of the week! As I write these words I utter a very simple prayer: God speak to me in dreams, take my dream life and use it.[22]

VISIONS

There is a biblical phenomenon, which is translated in the texts as 'vision'. I have used this word in the book so far as a descriptor of something that grips your life. I have implied that there is a spiritual purpose and goal to the vision that you have; there is something of your destiny wrapped up in it; there is something for you to attain under God. However, the meaning of the word 'vision' in biblical understanding carries a different, although not unrelated meaning.

Visions are part of a divine impartation of knowledge, understanding and prophetic utterance. They tend to be more literal than figurative; can seem to be real rather than allegorical. 'Vision', literally, is something that is gazed upon, something that you see (albeit with spiritual eyes), a sighting or appearance. In the Old Testament the prophets were sometimes called 'seers',[23] because of this visualising gift that they had. The prophet Isaiah refers to the visions that he saw at the beginning of his collected prophetic words.

Ezekiel, who clearly moved in a prophetic ministry, at the age of thirty had a heavenly open-eyed vision. He even dated the entry, in what we can assume is an extract from his journal. As we read his diary entry he describes, in detail, a vision of a storm approaching with thunder and lightning. Then it seems to move from a natural picture to a spiritual picture. He is grasping for words to describe the living creatures that he sees surfing the storm. They are human-like, with wings and four faces. Now, with our logical exegetical minds we seek to interpret this and understand, which I would agree is legitimate and proper. However, I think that in our bid to understand we miss the spiritual event, the moment of 'wow'. This young man was just recalling the amazing thing he saw; he wasn't trying to understand it fully, he wasn't trying to write a book.

He made some notes after the event to remember what had happened to him. A few chapters later he describes being 'lifted up by the Spirit'.[24] He was literally flying high above the scene; this guy was going for a ride.

When you suspend disbelief, suspend your sceptical mindset, stop trying to write a commentary and just experience the scene with Ezekiel, you get a whole new meaning. This is an account of a man telling you what he saw with his spiritual eyes; eyes that saw something so real that it could well have been with his natural eyes. He was literally peering into heaven and recounting his experience.

Now take it at face value. God wanted to speak to Ezekiel and show him what is happening in the realm called the 'heavenlies'. God has got his attention, can speak to him, give him directions, even utter mysteries that Ezekiel struggles to fathom. When Ezekiel landed, he describes walking away in *bitterness and turmoil, but the Lord's hold on me was strong.*[25] This guy was a mess! God had 'fried his circuits'. No wonder he could not get his head around what had happened. He had just had the heavenly tour and was trying to get his bearings — I should think he would be a little dazed!

This whole idea happens again in the New Testament with John in his holiday home on the Greek island of Patmos. (It actually says he was exiled. I think I could cope with being exiled on a Greek island!) John was worshipping in the Spirit. Suddenly, he was interrupted by a loud, resonant voice speaking to him, surrounded by candlesticks. The Son of Man, Jesus of course, starts telling him about some remarkable letters that needed to be written to the angels with responsibility for the Asian churches. Not surprisingly, John was flat on his face pretending to be dead! When he looks up, he sees the door with the invitation to come on up. Then he has the heavenly tour and is paraded with mystery mixed with history past and future. No wonder he refers to this as revelation.

Now why is it we get ourselves tied up in knots over the Book of Revelation? Because we are trying to apply earth-grounded intellect to heavenly experiences? Of course, interpretation has value; of course we should be able to study this stuff with our minds; and of course our minds have been given to us for this purpose. But I think that the tendency of modern man is to rely on the intellect and natural mind too much, and normally to the detriment of our spiritual life. We lock ourselves into rational explanations when we are capable of understanding heavenly mystery with our spirit which may not be able to be communicated with words.

You could perhaps think of a stirring piece of music that causes tears to flow. Do you respond because the notes have been arranged in a mathematical order that causes the emotion to be evoked? Get a life! There is something about the music that touches us with great passion; we understand the sentiment of the composer with something other than raw intellect. There is no perfect analogy, but we can see that there is at least a place for direct personal experience. But we are also to remember that we are commanded to love God with all our minds, as well as in the other ways, so I certainly don't mean stop using your mind. I do mean: don't restrict your thinking about what God is doing and revealing to what might seem probable according to a rationalistic mindset.

In Acts chapter 10 we see something of the way in which an authentic vision from God should be accepted and expected. It is 3 p.m., and the off duty officer of the elite army regiment gets a visitation. An angel comes towards him in a vision, giving him exact instructions on how to find some guy called Peter. Next day, Peter is having a rooftop aperitif, waiting for lunch to be served, reading the Joppa Chronicle and he falls into a trance. Now this seems at first glance to be 'not on', as it offends our evangelical sensibilities. 'Trances are for weirdoes — but it is in the Bible, so let's assume that it is a minor aberration and overlook it!'

Peter has an awesome vision that will impact the course of the early church. His vision of the sheet filled with non-kosher animals is about to rock a major doctrinal plank of the growing church movement. On one level, God was showing Peter that 'the Way' was for all and the old food regulations of the old covenant did not apply to Christians, whether they were Jews or Gentiles. Cornelius's staff arrive to invite Peter for a meeting, where Peter now realises that the Christ that he has been preaching is for anyone who will hear and respond, and not only for Jewish believers.

So how did this key doctrine of the church get introduced? In a trance! Now if today a church leader told his congregation that he was waiting for lunch and fell into a trance, he would get some funny looks. If he then added that God had told him to stop Sunday meetings and start evangelising the nightclubbers on Friday nights, the deacons would move in with a vote of no confidence, or the PCC might make demands of the bishop to remove this heretic! We have got ourselves so removed from authentic spiritual life that if someone falls into a trance they would be thought to need to see a psychiatrist! Can you see what has happened to the Western church? We have become so neutered, so insulated from the spectacular supernatural, so blunted, that the diversity and simplicity of the flow of God's voice has been removed. We have complicated something that should be straightforward. Now I am not suggesting that you make a new 'doctrine' out of your vision; you will need to test what you see with the Bible. The vision of the believer must always be in harmony with Scripture.

ANGELIC VISITATION

Some time ago people started to notice circles appearing on photographs, which were explained as being angels. Now my sceptical instincts immediately assumed that there was a problem with the camera or that this phenomenon should be dismissed as being nonsense. When circles started to appear on my photos I began to reappraise this slightly. It got me wondering, what are angels? And apart from adding spice to the Christmas story, do they have any relevance to today's church? I have heard people talk about seeing angels, and even my wife says that she can see them standing in the corner of our living room!

When heavenly stuff happens, angels seem to appear. They were present on Jacob's ladder, they were present at Christ's birth. The men in white tell the disciples of the return of Christ;[26] an angel opened the doors for the apostles,[27] and an angel told Philip where to go next.[28]

Key to our understanding of angels is the fact that they are described as ministering spirits.[29] The idea, which is developed in the Amplified Bible, is that they are sent out from God to serve and give assistance to those who are going to inherit salvation — a sort of heavenly rescue service! These guys are on a task from the Boss, with a job to do.

Elijah has an encounter with an angel.[30] Elijah is on the run from Jezebel, who is out to kill him. Eventually, he hides in a cave and tells God that frankly he has had enough —he just wants to die. Have you ever had one of those days? But God sends an angel to touch him and bake some fresh bread to revive him.

After falling asleep again, Elijah is awoken to eat some more. The angel is nursing him in order to get him to Horeb, God's mountain, where God speaks to Elijah and gives him fresh instructions. Have we clipped the wings of the angels with our fat baby images that we see in Renaissance paintings? I don't see any obese baby angels in Scripture — most of the time they are pretty fearsome body-builder types!

In Acts 5:19, and then later in Acts 12, there are miraculous jailbreaks. In the Acts 12 event, Peter is put in prison, so an angel suddenly appears and releases him. The angel gives Peter a quick kick, tells him to get up, and off they go. Peter, used to odd things by now, thinks it is a vision, but it is real, and when he comes to himself he realises that he is in the street outside the jail.

Angels often carry messages to man from God, announcing facts and making specific requests. Paul talks about the angel who told him that he would stand trial before Caesar.[31] The Gospel of Luke is full of angelic messages. Zechariah has a visit;[32] Mary gets the shock of her life,[33] and the shepherds are given an impromptu

concert.[34] Daniel got a visit from Gabriel,[35] giving him
a picture of end time matters so powerful that he was
exhausted with the revelation; he didn't really know
what to do with it. Later, the angel appeared again,[36]
and told Daniel that he came to give him 'insight and
understanding'. Daniel had another angelic encounter,[37]
ending up by receiving strength.

The final appearance of angels in Daniel's life is an
interesting account that shows us that angels are here
to reveal God's plans and purposes. When angels
bring you a message there is something binding and
permanent.[38] This is God meaning business, leaving
you no room for wriggling out of his plans. Even the
Old Testament law seems to have been delivered by
angels![39]

Why make a big deal of angels? Because the
pendulum has swung too much over to the side of
dismissing them. Angels are all over the Scriptures, but
they are not all over the church. Well, they are all over
the church, but we are too dull to see them! I don't want
to start going mad about angels, but shouldn't we expect
their appearance? Shouldn't they be part of the package
of God's visitation and communication with his church?
Has God pensioned off the angelic host because they are
not necessary today now that we have the presence of the
Holy Spirit, and the complete Bible, the word of God?

My cry is for the authentic, living church of Jesus Christ

to awaken the historic, tried and tested ways to hear God, so that we can walk with certainty in the knowledge that he is with us. Surely Christians need to stop moaning that we can't hear God clearly, and press into the ways which God seems to have given us to hear him. Can you imagine a church that flows daily with prophetic words and individual and corporate dreams and visions, with angels coming on Sunday as well as the congregation? Just imagine if Gabriel appears in the pulpit this Sunday, or you are given a warning to avert a family disaster, or you are eating your sandwich in the park at lunchtime and God takes you up into the heavenlies! Is this really the stuff of fantasy, unreality and the excesses of charismatic fanatics? Or is this biblical and able to help us live our lives with the power of heaven impacting the real world? Don't think of the voice of God as a vague impression, or as though there were a 'lottery' chance of hearing it. Hearing his authentic voice helps us to walk in and exercise victorious faith.

Eight

LIVING THE ADVENTURE

I wouldn't describe myself as a 'trekkie', but there is something evocative about the Star Trek music. Growing up with the adventures of Captain Kirk and the crew of the Enterprise as an intrinsic part of my childhood means that I feel as if I am ready to be beamed up at any time! John Eldredge remarks on our innate sense of adventure, the need to go on a hunt and search out unfamiliar territory, going boldly into places where others have not gone.[1] Now I am not a particularly macho man. Anyone who is reading this who actually knows me will be laughing at even the idea of my being macho. I am ginger-haired (that surely says it all!), wine and opera loving, and I will turn the TV off when the football is on and visit castles when on holiday. However, I have an intense desire for adventure, a need to search out possibilities; I tend to be looking for the next great opportunity; I am someone who loves the journey as much as the arrival. Whether adventure is physical, emotional, intellectual or spiritual, I think it is in us all, male or female. We are made for adventure, made for the travel that we undertake for our eighty or so years on this planet. Our very bodies are vehicles that navigate the pot-holed roads of life.

However, so many of us get stopped along the way. We start out well and then fall into a massive hole on the road. Try as we might, we never seem to move on. Something cuts in on us and closes us down. So here we sit, the adventurous spirit slowly draining away as the engine of life ticks over. We can stay in neutral for so long that we forget that we even have a gear that is designed to move us forward. But we are designed with a superb gearbox that will not merely get us inching forward, step by step, but will also allow us to steam full ahead with very little to stop us.

The other day I met someone I had not seen for many years. She tried to ignore me, and certainly wasn't going to approach me. I could see she was sitting there thinking, 'I wonder if he will talk to me; I know he has seen me.' Not the easiest person I have known, but I decided I would say hello. "Hi there," I said with my best pastor's smile. "How are you?" Oh, oh —a mistake if ever there was one. Now, would she play ball and give me the customary answer, 'fine', or would she actually tell me?

There was no 'hello' in return, no polite smile, but a,

"Do you really want to know?" —with a sharpness in her tongue. Oh no. I really did not have time to deal with any issues, I was on a very tight schedule and this was not the place for any intense conversation, so I replied with an, "Oh dear, well I just wanted to say hi," and I moved on fairly quickly. As I reflected on the incident I felt a deep sorrow for her. I knew of her difficult circumstances, and the hardship she has faced, but the thing that struck me was the fact that the dream had gone out of her eyes. Where once there was a spark of hope and optimism there was now nothing really. She had been driving along with hope, and had fallen into a deep pit with no exit ramp.

There is a little known chap in the Bible called Terah, the father of Abraham.[2] I think he fell into a bit of a hole somewhere along the way. Terah was a man who worshipped and served other gods apart from Jehovah,[3] and lived just outside Babylon in Ur of the Chaldeans. Terah had three sons: Haran (who died whilst they lived in Ur), Nahor and, of course, Abram (later to be called Abraham). Here is a picture of a people who are captive, held in a land for many generations — but it was not the place where Jehovah God wanted them. We see in the rest of the Old Testament that Babylon always figured as a place of captivity and not a place where God wants his people to settle. Now while the family is in Ur, God speaks. It is all a little confusing because the

Genesis account of God's call to Abram appears to be after the family leave Ur. However, the rest of Scripture suggests that Abram, perhaps even the family, had a call from God to leave Ur and go to Canaan, the symbol in Scripture of the promised land, the place of destination and fulfilment. Later in the New Testament, Stephen, under the inspiration of the Holy Spirit, tells us that 'the God of glory' appeared to Abraham whilst he was in Ur, telling him to leave his people group and country to go to a mystery land.[4] So let's assume it was something like this.

The family hits a crisis, which hits many families today, when the eldest son of Terah dies. A tragedy for any family when the child dies before the parents. This causes the family to reappraise where they are and what they want. Abram, who is a Jehovah worshipper, tells his father of the command of God to leave their homeland and go on a mystery tour. Well, Terah being a god-fearing man (although not a single God-fearing man) agreed and they set out for a different land —that of Canaan. The family gathered up everything that was theirs – servants, cattle, possessions – and set off, becoming a nomadic caravan in the desert, vaguely heading for somewhere. Terah, putting his trust in his son's ability to sense the guidance of the divine, is perhaps still grieving for his eldest son.

On their travels they came across a settlement which

was either called Haran,[5] or out of remembrance of the son that died they named it Haran. This was far enough for the old man. He was pretty weary — he was over two hundred years old, so frankly he had had enough! (Haran is an okay place, we'll stop here.) So the caravan took up permanent residence in Haran. Abram knew it wasn't the destination, but he stopped because the family stopped.

Well, it wasn't long before Terah died, there in Haran. After the funeral had taken place, God spoke again to Abram. This record we have in Genesis 12. God reiterates his intention for Abram to be the man of pilgrimage, a man who has to follow after something that is not seen in the natural and not mapped out. Abram is promised greatness, nationhood and blessing. God spells out to him that he is on his side and will curse anyone who curses him —pretty awesome, having Jehovah putting his weight behind Abram. So at the age of seventy-five – no spring chicken by modern standards – Abram sets off with wife, nephew, slaves and possessions towards Canaan.

Abraham was a man called and convicted by God with a heavenly vision.[8] It was by faith that Abraham obeyed when God called him to leave home and go to another land which God would give him as his inheritance. Abraham went without knowing where he was going.[9] And even when he reached the land God promised him, he lived there by faith—for he was like a foreigner, living in tents. And so did Isaac and Jacob, who inherited the same promise.[10] Abraham was confidently looking forward to a city with eternal foundations, a city designed and built by God. (See Hebrews 11:8–10, NLT).

Abraham operated by faith, whether he knew it theologically or not, believing in something that he couldn't see. He saw this incredible inheritance that was his. It was in the shape of a physical slice of the Middle East, although he clearly was 'seeing' at several levels. Yes, there was the land known as Canaan, but there was also something that he saw with his inner eye, his spiritual sight. This was an eternal city, a city that John in the New Testament has a tour of in his Patmos vision. God had gripped Abram. He had grabbed him, and nothing much was going to shake the hand of God from his life. To me, this is what a true heavenly calling and vision is. You are grabbed and compelled to follow something that makes little sense with our limited human understanding and intellect, but makes complete sense when the human spirit is impacted by the Holy Spirit.

Abram was a responder to the heavenly call to adventure. He embraced the life of faith, the journey of the pilgrim, following something that he could taste with his spiritual taste buds. Abram was a pursuer, the promised land was in his heavenly gaze, and he was going for it. When he was somewhere en route to the land of his dreams, he 'built an altar to the Lord' near Bethel.

This was a man who was set on following his God and would not bottle out or settle for second-best.

Abram wasn't moving out of frustration or out of rebellion. No, he had a relationship with the living God, and was responding to the voice of his heavenly Father. Many of the people of God act presumptuously out of frustration, or even rebellion. Consider the number of church splits and church plants that are birthed out of a frustrated spirit. Of course they can all be redeemed, so if that's you, don't sit under a cloud of rejection throwing this book into the bin out of anger, rather get on your knees, ask the Father to guide your prayers, and repent! That is something we all need to do. As soon as something nasty in our lives raises its head, repent! After repentance God graciously gives forgiveness, from which flows healing and restoration.

How many of us are just like Terah? We respond to some sort of call – probably second-hand – and go out on it only to get sidetracked and end up living in a land that we never intended to. I cannot tell you whether Terah should have stayed in Ur or not, but what I am pretty convinced about is that he never had the vision to go to the promised land — that was for Abram. Now, of course you can follow another's vision. Leaders, after all, should set out a picture that others may embrace. But a vision must become your vision if it is to be long-term, or you will probably settle in a lay-by.

LEADING A TEAM

Good leaders know how to communicate a God-inspired vision in such a way that it becomes a shared vision. Thankfully, I think the day of one-man band leadership is drawing to an end. We need to grasp the idea that 'team' can be central to God's purposes. God does raise up individuals for particular tasks, but we are shown in the New Testament a good deal about 'the body' and complementarity in ministry. Teamwork should not imply compromise or weakness; there is a team dynamic where someone may have been entrusted with the root vision, but it is truly a shared vision. I have done the one-man band leadership thing and frankly got exhausted.

When I was in business I was pretty much the boss because it was my business. I would have the big idea and off we went pursuing what I wanted to do. It was my money, my idea, my business! Now sometimes we were successful, but actually, with hindsight, we made more mistakes than I would like to admit, and they actually cost me money and my business – my ego took quite a bashing.

On taking up church leadership, I realised fairly early on that the same entrepreneurial style of leadership had some merits but actually wasn't going to last in the long run. There are seasons when being entrepreneurial is a great way of making something happen (in my view, the church has often become a stagnant pond because of the lack of momentum created by reactive leadership), but in the seasons of maturing, the church leadership must grow up to embrace the concepts of a culture that empowers people to live the dream that is in their heart.

Nowadays, when I get the next big idea I am not too quick to share it with everyone, because I realise that not everyone can cope with ideas. If I share the latest God-inspired vision too soon it can have the opposite effect from releasing and empowering. A half-baked idea can cause many people to become frustrated because I haven't considered all the practical implications, or they get 'paralysed' because it is just too huge to contemplate at the moment.

My wife and I have had to work on this one in our marriage. There was a time when I would share an idea and she would list all the 'buts', which in turn would frustrate and anger me because I felt that she was ripping my idea to shreds, whereas she was just being practical. Now we try to give each other space – she lets me talk my way into and out of an idea. Not every idea is a heavenly inspired idea. If you are an ideas person you will have twenty fresh inspirations before breakfast! They need chewing and maturing before they are ready to be classed as workable ideas. Many will flow from the inspiration of the Holy Spirit. After all, Creator God just spoke and stuff was created; he really is the source of all godly concepts and ideas, and we are truly created to be creative.

I often find that I get a passion for all sorts of kingdom enterprises and projects. Most of them are not for me to pursue, but rather for me to encourage in others. As a leader, my job is to fan into flame other people's imaginations, other people's dreams, getting the people of God to see that they can actually do it! I have learnt the hard way about getting knocked back and then getting up and having another go. But now I see that God has put in my heart a few divinely appointed mandates for me to do —my job, my call. The rest of the ideas are so that I can encourage others, seek out talent, release people, lift the lid on people's God-given creative ability.

Jesus taught on this with a story. We are all gifted with the ability to reproduce something. God has made man a producer, not just a consumer. In the story, as I like to paraphrase it, the successful entrepreneur goes away for a long time and sets his apprentices a task.[6] He assesses their gifts and abilities and then gives them some cash (the Bible translators decided to translate the original word 'talent'), expecting them to make a return on it. The apprentices get on with the job of making a return on the investment. When he calls them into the board room, two of them have doubled the investment through their imagination, hard work and energy. The result for both of them is 'a share in the boss's happiness'. But look at the way he deals with the weakest of the group. The third man is full of excuses, he was so terrified that he took the cash and just put it in a shoe box under his bed until his boss returned. He did absolutely nothing! So he sits with the others in the board room, takes out the shoe box and says, 'It's all here, untouched'. The boss is furious. 'You could have at least put it in a building society to get some interest! YOU'RE FIRED!'

Money in our lives means time, effort, substance, ability, so you can apply the story in the same way to us today. If cash is what you have, then for goodness sake use it to extend and expand the kingdom of God! But let's say it's your gifts and talents. It's quite useful that the translators left this word alone because God has gifted us all with skills that only we have. You may have many skills or just one, the story is the same. It's not what you start out with, it's what you do with them. I think the church of God squanders its talents. We have huge numbers of people who are not using what God has given them. Have *you* put a lid on *your* talent, never to use it again? What have you done with your dream, your vision, the thing that God has called you to? Is it in a box under your bed? Be under no illusion, God will want an explanation for what we have done, or not done, with what we have been given.

This story is sandwiched between the story of the ten virgins – five of whom were locked out of God's presence because they fell asleep and didn't have the necessary oil – and the story of the sheep and goats. All three stories are about judgement —something that we are not very good at talking about in case it upsets us! But let's make the message very clear. What are you doing with what God has given you to do? What are you doing with the deposit or gift that he has entrusted to you? Now if you are reading this and feeling condemned, it is very simple. There is not much separating one talent from two talents. In fact, the number of talents is not really the point of the story, it's about what you DO with them! Why not decide right now to do something with what God has given you? Put the book down and ask for forgiveness that you have done nothing much with what he has given you, and pray for opportunities to use your God-given gifting. If you can't think of what you are gifted with, may I suggest that you just serve the first need that you come across? That's like the boss's suggestion that you at least put the money in the bank and get interest.

SETTLING FOR SECOND BEST

Settling for second best is something that the church has become quite expert on. Life can get so consuming, so intense, so full that we just settle where we are at. We end up starting well with all good intentions, but somehow it is easy to get sidetracked. Life can do that, we can be full on for God, then get married, have kids, get promotion – effectively settle! Now I am not trying to suggest that those things are even wrong – no, of course not. Get married, have kids, get promotion, but DON'T SETTLE. Settling is a state of mind, something in your spirit. Settling is where we allow ourselves to become dull and lifeless, where we allow the spark of the vision to fade away into a distant youthful memory of something that God said a long time ago. It is not true that life has to get on top of you to the point that you lose your vision and energy.

Paul gets at this idea when he asks the question, *Who cut in on you and kept you from obeying the truth?*[7] He was a pretty firm sort of apostle, not someone who minced his words. I like Paul because he speaks out clearly God's word on the matter: *Throw off everything that gets in the way.*[8] If it is going to slow you down, then strip it off; if you have to run naked in order to run the path set out for you then do it. (Please, I am not advocating a 'naturist

Christianity', it is just a figure of speech to make the point!) I suppose what I am calling for is a gut-wrenching, raw grit type of faith that will follow whatever God has spoken to you about. We have such a 'domesticated' and 'civilised'[9] (and I would say, 'watered-down') faith. We have become slick, well-marketed, efficient at what we do, but I wonder if we have lost the fundamental grittiness of the authentic Christian experience.

When Moses went out into the desert, God gave fresh bread and fresh meat every day. Now my entrepreneurial instinct would be to want to produce a range of manna products. Manna sliced, manna light, manna rolls, crusty manna, manna in packs of four, ten and maxi manna! Then I would be onto the incredible line of pies and stews made from quail! But God told the people to just take enough for today . . . . TODAY! What was that about? I wonder whether as believers we are trying to feed off yesterday's manna. The idea is that you get faith fresh today, and it is yours and not something borrowed or remembered. Many believers are living off yesterday's revival, historic teaching, traditional practices, that cannot suffice and fill them. You are eating mouldy manna! I am all for digging up our historic roots, exploring new forms of worship, reading about past revivals, finding life in age-old traditions – but find the newness in it. Part of the decay that the church finds itself in is because it lives on leftovers.

I hate leftover food. It is one of my funny quirks. When I get the munchies at about 9 p.m., and a movie is on television, I go foraging for supplies in the kitchen. My darling wonderful wife will say to me, "There is leftover pasta in the fridge." My heart sinks, my craving for food will never be satisfied with leftover anything. Give me a packet of red onion and cheddar crisps, but leftover pasta makes me want to fast! Why, oh why, do we settle for leftover faith? Why do we go to our church fridges and eat what is old? Probably because there is nothing new in the house —the weekly shop has not been done and you are down to the dregs. Stop settling for second-rate, second best, old used-up faith! It is yuk in food and yuk in faith!

TIME TO GET OFF THE SOFA

As much as we would like to live out our adventures through other people, there comes a point where you will need to stop what you are doing and do something different. You will never fulfil the call of God on your life if you continue to do the same things. Why not challenge yourself to think . . . .

- *What has God actually called me to? If you can't think of anything ask yourself: 'What dreams did I have long ago which have become distant memories?'*

- *If I were actually to do something about the call of God how would my life need to change? What am I doing now that is stopping God's plan from coming about in my life?*

- *Is my job the right sort of job for me?*

- *Am I living in the right place?*

- *Am I being fully used and challenged in my local church?*

- *Am I practising being a servant in my church?*

- *Am I making right choices with my money?*

- *Do my friendships and relationships encourage me to pursue God's call on my life?*

- *What about your thinking? Is it healthy? Do you think in line with your vision, or is your mind pursuing another agenda?*

- *What do you feed your mind on — things that will enhance it or things that destroy it?*

> You cannot expect to live in line with the vision God has given you if you have wrong thinking

The mind is a battleground, and changing your mindset can be a huge hurdle. You may not be able to change it on your own and may need help to do this. You need to be steeped in the word of God, let your thinking be renewed by the word, and have the mind of Christ.

Emotionally, how are you? Are you fragile and susceptible to criticism and comment? Do you find yourself overly sensitive to others? Could you cope with rejection and disappointment? Do you have the emotional strength to pursue God's vision?

What do you want to do? Is your response: 'Actually, when all is said and done, I am happy living the way I have always lived and I don't want to really be bothered'? Sadly, that would be the honest answer for many believers. We would rather settle in compromise than press ahead to the finishing post. God doesn't usually cross the line called our will. He gives us a great measure of freedom to make choices. He may have spoken to you about a dream, but it will remain totally unfulfilled if you don't do anything about it. You are, in one sense, free to remain a 'couch potato Christian', just consuming your spiritual food like a locust – ever eating and never satisfied. I would suggest to you that you will never be satisfied until you begin living the adventure. Much more important than our own satisfaction and fulfilment, though, there is a danger that we become like the servant about whom Jesus spoke in the parable, who failed to use his 'talent'. It is vital that our heart's desire, our vision, our will, our actions, should be in line with his purpose for us; and that we should be fruitful disciples, abiding in him and doing his will in the kingdom.

Living the adventure means making a change to the ordinary things of life: what you do, what you think, how you feel. A life of adventure needs you to decide to change something, on the basis of God's word, to realise the dream or vision he gives.

Nine

STAYING ON TRACK

One of the problems of pursuing a vision concerns your ability to keep on track. It's all very well getting a 'grand plan' and making life decisions on that plan, but what happens when you feel that you have lost the plot and the vision seems so far away? A walker can stand at the top of a hill and see the destination in the distance; you know you have to cover a lot of ground to get there, but you can do it because you can observe what lies ahead. However, when you are in the valley, with hills on each side, up to your ankles in mud and fighting your way through overgrown paths, the destination seems a long way off; you need to be motivated to keep pressing ahead to get to the goal. Somehow you need to have that vision burned on the inside; what you saw must have a lasting residue in your very soul, or otherwise, frankly, you are going to give up!

Achieving the vision that God has put in your heart will

take perseverance, tenacity and grit. It is not all just going to happen (not exactly words of encouragement!) Most of my experiences in the Christian walk have required some determination. I am not talking about a 'works' type of determination, but the sort that Paul talks about when he describes running in a race and setting out to win the prize.[1] This isn't about lots of effort to prove ourselves before God, but rather determination to run after everything that God is calling us to.

So how do you stay on track when everything around you seems to be trying to prevent you from fulfilling what has been imprinted on your heart? How do I keep my eyes on the heavenly vision, my goal and aim?

Through whom [Jesus] *also we have access by faith into this grace in which we stand, and rejoice in hope of the glory of God* (Romans 5:2, NKJV).

The theology of this verse gives us a methodology that we can apply to our lives when we feel the vision draining away from us. This verse will help when we feel drained of all hope, when we are fed up with life not turning out how we thought it would, when the amazing vision for our lives seems like just a fantasy!

Believers have the power and opportunity to reshape their lives and circumstances to come in line with the heavenly picture. Faith is the vehicle for that, hope is the rope that secures us, and love is the means by which we receive and give away.

The object of the verse is the glory of God. This is the very place where God is, the place that we first saw the vision he entrusted us with, the very throne room of heaven, the place where heavenly plans are hatched and despatched to willing believers. The glory of God is the presence of God, his radiance, his will. The glory is the cloud that consumed the Israelites in the desert, the fire that spoke to Moses, the cloud that filled the temple, which caused all the priests to fall over. The glory made Isaiah feel unworthy, impacted Ezekiel, and led to John being caught up in a vision! The vision that we carry, if it is authentically from God, if it originated in the courts of the King, will glorify him.

This verse in Romans teaches us about getting access to his glory. We are admitted into the divine palace and introduced to the King of kings. As the Father's adopted kids, we have the privilege of gaining access to him whenever we want. Gone are the stuffy days when children were seen but seldom heard, when father's study was a sanctuary free from childish interference, and gone too are the religious days when sacrifice and offerings gave us access just a few times a year, where the priest was the only one who could get access to God. Yes! Jesus makes it absolutely clear that in him *we have boldness and access with confidence through faith in Him* (Ephesians 3:12, NKJV). If it is true that I have a heavenly Father, then I relate to him as a son relates to a father. He may be King of kings but he is still my Father. I don't make my children knock on the door of my study! Whilst I am writing this, one of my daughters has come and is sitting next to me on the sofa, munching an apple in my ear! Leaning her head on my shoulder, she remarks, "You type fast", then proceeds to laugh at something that she has found funny! That is the type of relationship that we have with the King of kings, one that gives us access whenever we want.

ACCESS BY FAITH

But our access is 'by faith' — that certainty of the thing that you hope for, that surety of the thing that you do not see.[2] Abraham, the father of all believers,[3] pretty well grasped this concept. He came to a place of believing that God can create something out of nothing. Abraham would have known the stories of creation, how God brought physical matter into being out of nothing, just by a word. Well, he also knew it in his life. God had been on his case about being famous and being a blessing to the nations;[4] then God started telling him that he would have a permanent land to dwell in,[5] which he would pass on to subsequent generations. Now all this was okay, but then God started to point to the stars and suggest that Abraham and Sarah were going to have so many descendants that they would not be able to count them.[6] Now this was getting a bit near the bone because, of course, they didn't have any children and were not able to have children either. This seemed impossible!

Sometimes when we are faced with impossibilities we try to work them out so that they won't be impossible. Let's say you are faced with a financial problem and there seems no way out. Well, you can sort it out by taking a loan, working overtime or inheriting from a relative – there are lots of ways to overcome the problem. Now I am all for people doing their best to work out the problem. God is pleased to reward our diligence and hard work, but when faced with an impossible situation, what do we do? Give up the dream, postpone the idea for the time being and let the situation change?

Sarah had an idea. Why not marry her servant, Hagar, and have a child through her. Excellent idea! Abraham was up for it. (That will give us an heir and then the promise of God will be fulfilled through him.) Well this is what they did, and the child's name was Ishmael. Actually, it was a pretty good plan, but it was not God's plan. You can devise a scheme and work out a solution, but if it is not an idea from God then it is not going to be the solution to the impossible situation that you face. Now God often does honour our plans. Ishmael was loved, and God spoke a great word over him,[7] but he was not what God had planned for Abraham. God wanted Abraham and Sarah to have a miracle baby. When we meet the impossible, and the 'word' that God spoke into our lives seems ridiculous, we can produce 'Ishmaels' in an attempt to force God's hand. Let's face it, God does take his time, and for people who like things today, sometimes God seems to them to be a little too slow. (I don't mean to be blasphemous: his timing is really always perfect, whether we are aware of that along the way or not.)

Once you have overcome the barrier of embracing impossibility, you operate in the realm of the mountain-moving faith that Jesus talked about. He meant what he said! We might say, on one level, that faith is like a key that Jesus gives us. But it is important to note what that does not mean. Jesus and the apostles never suggest that it is a 'mechanical' thing, nor that it puts us back in the driving seat where Jesus should be. A 'slot machine' attitude is wrong because faith-based action is always to be based on our *relationship* with him, not about a mechanism for me getting whatever it is I happen to want. The disciples were being taught by Jesus how to exercise faith —taught by him, the Lord with whom they walked and talked and whom they were following. Of course it was all about what they were being instructed to do and ask for *in his name* (i.e. according to his will, under his authority, and in his power and strength). And we are meant to be abiding in him, operating under his lordship, and in line with the guidance of the Spirit. So it's not like putting a card in a machine and seeing money come out of the other slot! Operating by faith is relational, and there are principles Jesus taught, but always remember that he taught them relationally, and we recall too that teaching in John 14 about abiding in him. The principles of faith nowhere license us to act as independent operators!

INTO GRACE

Now just in case you feel completely condemned because I have made out that you need super faith to believe in the midst of impossible situations – don't fret! I am not saying that you need to be a superhero, just that your trust needs to be simple enough for you to believe God when he says something to you.

One of the things I have always loved doing with my kids is to fool them into believing me. They are pretty canny about my tricks now, and most of the time they don't believe me . . . um, perhaps I have taught them the wrong stuff; I'd better reconsider my strategy! However, the point is that children tend to take things at face value. I suppose that is why Jesus taught that our attitude to kingdom stuff should be very much like that of a child – keep it simple.

But what is faith for? Romans chapter 5 tells us about 'access into grace'. Essentially, grace is God's undeserved favour, the blessing of God that has been given even though we do not deserve it. This is the place that is devoid of condemnation, a place where guilt doesn't figure, a place where we can go when we feel lousy because, by definition, it is a place which is for people who don't deserve it. That's the point of grace, it is for people who really haven't saved up enough righteousness points to get there by merit — and that means all of us. We are given the grace (free gift) of entering into that place of adopted sonship by the free gift from God, the death of his Son, Jesus, on the cross for the forgiveness of our sin, and we can enter it only by repentance and faith in Jesus. That is what happened when you were born again by the Spirit of God.

Now when you are in pursuit of the vision and call of God and you mess up big time, what do you do? Well, I suggest that you run back to that place called grace. Remember the simple faith God gave you when he first brought you into his kingdom. Remember again the first time he gave you that saving faith which enabled you to turn to him in the first place, repenting and believing, and remember again that faith needs to be exercised all the time as trust and expectancy. It began by making you a new creation; it is then also about going on believing, going on trusting, going on abiding in him, and that covers everything you need to do and believe about the vision he has entrusted to you. It all comes under the umbrella of grace (gift) and it never stops being about faith (trust in him, and expectancy that he will do what he has said he will do).

The problem about grace is that it is so simple that actually we often don't get it. We make it out to be more complex than it really is. But if more of us got the idea of grace, then we wouldn't go on beating ourselves up nearly as much for our failures, after we have repented and received God's forgiveness. If you look at the characters in the Bible there seems to be a common thread — they were a real shower of failed holy people.

Abraham, the so-called father of faith, pretended Sarah was his sister to save his own skin; Jacob conned his brother out of his birthright; David had a monumental failing; Peter denied he ever knew Jesus; and Paul actively persecuted and killed early believers ... um, let me see, would I put any of these people on my leadership team? But what qualified them? They gained access to this wonderful, never-ending grace of God through faith in him. They simply believed. I don't really know how to make this any plainer; it is so simple it is offensive to our rational minds. The plain fact is that there is a permanent open way for you to come to Father in heaven, in repentance and faith, no matter how many times you have messed up. And that is because of his grace, his one free gift of the death and resurrection of Jesus Christ, once given.

Some criticise this approach, saying it is 'cheap grace', the idea that you can keep sinning and repenting, the cycle of 'sin – repent – sin – repent'. But the cross was not cheap, it cost God what was most precious, and we must go on remembering that.

So often in society we seem to be held in a trap from which we can't escape. But I am compelled by my reading of Scripture to conclude that the New Testament is clear: grace is available for us all the time, if we have faith and repent. If we approach mistakes and sin from a grace perspective, then any judgemental, critical, harsh spirit is wiped out of our own attitudes towards others, because we begin to realise how much and how graciously we have been forgiven by God. The process of getting free from the stuff that slows us down begins. In a judgemental atmosphere we will never get free from anything. We will just feel shame, and hide!

If we want to be a people operating in our gifts, pursuing the vision that God has given us, then we have to be a people who experience the heart of the Father —his grace. We are saved by his grace,[8] find strength in grace,[9] and we find that what we actually need to keep on course is grace.[10] Even though we are weak, God's grace is powerful. As we truly plumb the depths of grace, he puts a desire for holiness in us. If you don't find this to be so, then I am not sure you have truly experienced God's saving grace. I think The Message puts this idea wonderfully— *and that's not all: We throw open our doors to God and discover at the same moment that he has already thrown open his door to us* (Romans 5:2, The Message). It is a wonderful thing about grace that God has opened his door to us so widely.

STAND IN IT

Sometimes we forget to stand in grace, normally because we stop believing. Shame and guilt are cleverly designed to boot you out of the awareness of God's grace and to unsettle you. They suggest to us that we can't receive God's forgiveness, and remind us that actually we deserve to be punished. Well, in one sense they are correct. That is actually what we do deserve. But shame and guilt over sins for which we have repented and which have been forgiven can mean we are doubting what God has done for us. A sense of condemnation may then weigh heavily on us.

Years ago there used to be a programme called Gladiators. As a family we loved it, because competitors would fight the muscle-laden body-builders and earn points. Well, one game had a gladiator and contender fighting with a stick, with foam pads, on a twenty-foot tower. They had to knock each other off their platform to win the game. What if you were the contender standing on that tower? This reminds me about grace: you may not deserve to be where you are, but you are put high on a tower which is held up by God. Then along comes this brute of a gladiator and with one swipe you are tumbling to the ground —shame has come along and knocked you off your perch. You start to think you didn't belong there anyway; you are puny, with no muscle and wonder why are you involved. That's what shame does, bam, it knocks you off the perch that you don't even belong on! But the good contenders have a bit of an attitude. When Mr Muscle comes along to knock them off the perch, they swing back. Effectively they are saying, 'Get lost shame. You may be right, I may be puny, I may be weak, I may not deserve to be here, but I am staying here on the perch where my God has put me!' Stand in the grace.

As Christians we can be pathetic. Along comes an accusation and we get knocked over again. Well, get up and stand! How are you going to see the word of God fulfilled in your life if you don't get up and stand in the grace of God? When we start resisting shame, accusation and fear, then we are standing in the grace.

'To stand' here means, literally, to establish, stand still, be on standby. If you are on standby you are waiting for something to happen; you are alert, positioned in a posture of readiness. Why are we always so surprised when we get hit? You make progress with your vision, things fall into place, you are encouraged and then WHAM

– you get hit by a force! It always seems to come when we don't expect it. Hey, go figure! There is a spiritual force out there that is out to knock you around and get you off course. If you are not standing in the grace spot, then you are not going to see your dream come about. That is why the Bible tells us to get prepared with armour.[11] You don't need armour for a walk in the park, you only need it if you are in a war! When evil comes at you (let's include shame in that), stand your ground and check that your armour is in place —then what? Well, stand! Once we have found our way into the place of freedom, the place of God's grace, we don't want to leave. Once we have tasted of heavenly delight, been captured by the upward call of God —frankly I want to stay in that place of grace. Well, you've got there by being simple enough just to believe it — so stand in it.

It is for freedom that Christ has set us free. Stand firm, then, and do not let yourselves be burdened again by a yoke of slavery (Galatians 5:1, NIV).

Look, this isn't rocket science. It's not supposed to be. This is supposed to be something that we can all get hold of. Stick at it; stand in the grace of God.

REJOICE IN THE HOPE

Hope has a pretty odd meaning in our modern world. We talk about dreamy, magical hope: 'I hope one day to go to Disneyland'; 'I hope to be qualified one day'; 'I hope I win the lottery'. This is not what biblical hope is. We want to turn a 'wishing' hope into certain hope. Wishing hope is about a pursuit of our desires and wants based on our aspirations, and is not rooted in heavenly reality.

Certain hope is about pursuing a God-birthed destiny based on the evidence of faith. Get rid of any idea of a namby-pamby, pre-packaged hope that society dishes up. That is not biblical hope. That is not the hope that will never fail you; that is the hope that will always disappoint you, always fall short of what was promised in the glossy brochure.

When we set out into our dream, when we give up all to respond to the call of God, we will lose our way if what we live for is never realised. The Message says, *unrelenting disappointment will make us sick and fed up with our lot.*[12] We are not created to continually defer that which is promised; delay produces disillusionment and disappointment. I see many believers who have believed passionately for a future and have got worn out by unfulfilled expectations. A revival culture can do that. We believe, rightly, for revival, and when it doesn't happen we give up with fatigue. A heavenly inspired vision is not a promise of something that is vague, a hope that 'one day' you will achieve it, but rather vision is a picture that we can grasp and see happen. A heavenly inspired vision may paint a 'difficult picture'; it may show obstacles that seem like mountains in our sight, an outrageous impossibility. But once you have grasped this sort of vision, you feel that you can scale any obstacle! Vision is unstoppable, with hope that is rooted in heaven; vision is unobtainable without hope. Your vision is too great to scale, too wide to get around, unless you have hope. Hope provides the footing, hope provides the hook that can catch us if we fall, that can hold our weight when we have lost our bearings.

The church, over the years, has all too often exchanged a certain, reliable, dependable hope for a 'cross your fingers' wish only realised by a few 'lucky' souls. Biblical hope includes the absolute conviction of being raised from the dead,[13] the gospel,[14] glory,[15] salvation,[16] our calling,[17] eternal life,[18] and the realisation of the promise made to our fathers.[19] Hope is good, living, blessed and better.[20] This is anything but a media-inspired frenzy of wishful thinking! Hope absolutely holds us fast to the vision of heaven; it is a rope that keeps us held fast and firm.

This hope we have as an anchor of the soul, both sure and steadfast, and it enters the presence behind the veil (Hebrews 6:19, NKJV).

Do we regularly refresh our hope, keep it alive, keep it real, keep it fresh? So much about the reality of our hope runs away from us. It gets buried in the business of life, it gets dulled by the weight of concern. But if we want to stay on track we need hope.

The lines of purpose in your lives never grow slack, tightly tied as they are to your future in heaven, kept taut by hope. The message is as true among you today as when you first heard it. It doesn't diminish or weaken over time (Colossians 1:5, *The Message*).

Your life purpose is birthed in heaven. It is heavenly inspired. So then to maintain it you need to hook it continually to heaven. Hope fuels your vision. Let your hope go and you will be running on empty, with no motivation to pursue it. Hope generates action —makes us walk towards the end goal. Hope is the focus of our aim, the bull's-eye of the vision. Vision without hope will mean we fall short of the objective; it means we will give up.

Faith gets us into that place where we can see and experience the heavenly plan for our lives. It is hope that cements that connection with heaven; hope that makes permanent what we have seen by faith. Once we have gained access by faith, then it is hope that sustains us. Hope is unseen[21] (like faith; God operates with the unseen as well as the seen).

Now, you want sticking power to stay the course —well

turn up the key verse in Romans 5— *And not only that, but we also glory in tribulations, knowing that tribulation produces perseverance; and perseverance, character; and character, hope. Now hope does not disappoint, because the love of God has been poured out in our hearts by the Holy Spirit who was given to us* (Romans 5:3–4, NKJV).

The product of trial and perseverance and character development is the formation of true 'hope' in us. Something is created inside us, something that will not fail us, disappoint, or be hollow or let us down. Hope is ultimately formed through the pains and knocks of life, and we know that our hope will not have been in vain because we experience daily the love of God poured out in our lives by the Holy Spirit. When you feel that you are about to give up because you have seen nothing, or have been knocked off the 'grace spot', consider that true hope is only formed in the pressure cooker of life. You know you have a hope that will hold you when the pressure is really on. Don't give up. Hope is getting formed on the inside of you.

Why don't you just grab hope, like a lifeline, a lifebelt? It keeps us from sinking into all the stuff of life that would snuff out the heavenly vision in us. Hope is attached to a secure place. It is not the stuff of someone's fanciful imagination; it is not just a nice story, read to children at bedtime; hope is actual, real, true, solid and dependable.

Hebrews says that hope is sure and steadfast and can be traced all the way to behind the veil. It enters the 'presence', the very place of God's dwelling. It is hooked onto something very firm and secure. Hope stops us from drifting, keeps us secure, and focuses us on where we go. So, through the door of heaven you find the rope of the anchor tying the soul to heaven, keeping us firmly set on course, held in a heavenly direction.

When hope vanishes, vision perishes. When this happens, we operate with religious shadows. We continue with the routine ritual rather than pursuing a vision of life and reality. When hope is around, we become bold,[22] we are full of life and energy. We need to dip into our hope daily; we need a sip of hope to refresh us for the longer journey. And hope has immediate impact. Hope keeps us going like an energy drink. Feed your hope, renew hope daily, set your hope above. Hope has to empower, invigorate and encourage us today.

So, when it gets pretty nasty, when you want to give up, grasp this principle:

- *We access by faith*
- *the grace of God*
- *in which we stand*
- *rejoicing in the hope of the glory of God*

Confidence can make the difference between defeat and success. We often doubt our faith and lose confidence in the unseen world of faith —be confident. We find it hard to recognise God's unfailing grace —be confident. We get knocked about and fall out of grace —get up and be confident. We don't really feel that our hope is secure —be confident!

When you are pursuing your dream, life is really tough. But turn your thinking around. If all your circumstances are closing in on you, this is an opportunity to develop heavenly hope —that will make a difference.

I have encouraged you to persevere in this. But all along the way, be aware that you are not alone. God is at work, and close to you. The hope that is yours is a gift of the Holy Spirit. You have received grace – having been given the greatest gift. It is the Lord who gives the victory. Though you need to persevere, the results don't all depend on you.

Ten

A BIGGER VISION

There is a trend that TV programme makers have captured at the moment. It is the idea about turning your dream into a reality. Our Saturday night television is full of talent shows, where the armchair critic is exposed to the journeys of hundreds of hopefuls to find the one winner. We have seen the journeys of pop singers, dancers, ice skaters, garden designers, ambitious apprentices and business entrepreneurs, who all vie for the attention of the judges. Just as in the Roman arenas of old, it is the people who decide whether the contenders get the thumbs up, or the thumbs down. Yes, your vote really counts!

There is a deep desire that we all have to perform and succeed at some level. We want – perhaps even need – to bring the dream that we harbour in our souls out into the open, and have a chance to see it become a reality.

However, when we have shared the momentary joy of the winner and seen the tears of the loser what are we left with? Are we galvanised and motivated to make a difference, to follow the dream? Or do we carry on with the humdrum aspects of life, happy to have shared in someone else's experience of living the dream? I think these programme makers may inspire some to go for it, but in the main they anaesthetise us; we merely live out the pretence of making our dreams a reality.

The people of God, the church, have done exactly this, in my view. We go to the service and listen to the sermon. But what do we do with it? Are we going to go soberly about our day-to-day business? Or, are we going to throw off the shackles of sobriety and pursue the vision?

This isn't really a 'how to have a vision' book, it is a 'poke' to live life a different way. As I write, I am screaming at the page to find words that will be such a provocation that they will cause the army of the people of God to get up, move out! We are supposed to be a people on the move, a transient people who are just passing through this world. We are a people who have got a mission and mandate from the King of kings, yet we have so easily settled, so easily conformed, and so easily become like all the other people around us.

JOURNEY TO PILGRIMAGE

Abraham has figured fairly prominently in this book because of his vision-motivated journey. He was the human founder of the Jewish nation,[1] which was the beginning of God's community of faith, a holy people, and the church of Jesus Christ. Abraham is the spiritual father of all those who have faith,[2] so his is a tremendous pattern for us.

Abram sets out on a journey that takes him from Ur to Canaan, with an interlude along the way. He sets out from the land that is sterile, a place with no future. Sarai's barrenness mirrors the life that they had there. Hear God's word to you? As the people of God we are designed to be on the move; we are supposed to be a pioneer people, a frontier people. As we set out on the journey, a powerful biblical principle comes into play —that the Creator God is able to bring something out of nothing. That is what he does with his chosen people. You may feel as if you have settled, yet you feel you are created for more. You may feel that you have absolutely nothing to give. The fact is that you are in a good place for God to operate in his creative power.

Abram gets a call from God to go to a land that God is going to show him, and he is confronted by a choice. He can move on this word of God to go to a mystery land. God doesn't give him a glossy housing development brochure entitled 'Canaan Towers', showing him all the delights of this land. No, he expects Abram to rely on what he has said to him. When God speaks, suddenly there is freedom for the future —if we have a word from God, then its fulfilment, of course, is possible, with him. Abram is given the means of escaping the hopelessness of his situation, he can stay where he is or turn back. Turn back to what? Barrenness? Staying safe means remaining barren; to leave the land, even with risk, is to have hope. Turning one's back on the place of barrenness is a powerful theme; it may signal 'repentance', a turning away from the things that marked the past to a new future in the way God has planned.

Too often we have reduced the gospel to something 'safe'. We have lost the edge of risky faith and decided to settle into what we know. When we try to find safety and security we stop becoming a people on a journey. We slow down, and we become a people who have stopped; we settle and we inhabit. Now don't misunderstand, I am not suggesting that we all need to move house and leave our churches in order to be a people on a journey. Even though our physical territory may be static, we should live our lives as a people of movement. I have lived in the same city for over twenty years and I feel that I am on a journey — I am on the move; I am not settling. I may have settled geographically (in fact I feel spiritually 'placed' in my city), but I still live in pursuit of something that I have seen in my spirit.

BEING GRIPPED

Perhaps 'journey' is not really the right word to describe what I feel — 'pilgrimage' would be closer. To me, pilgrimage is a journey, but with passion and objective. I am not just a nomad, moving aimlessly from one pastureland to another. No, I am a man on a mission. What was it that gripped me to mission and pilgrimage? To be honest, I can't actually think of any one moment or event. I think it was a spiritual gripping of God.

I remember one very dark day a few years ago, a moment when I felt completely empty and bereft of any sense of purpose or vision. I felt that I wanted out of family, business, church and of course, God! I had a moment when I felt as if I was on the edge of an abyss looking down. I was looking at a future of barrenness with no hope; I wasn't looking forward, I was looking down. I cannot really describe this event fully, but I felt a hand reach into me and pull me back from the edge. I remember it now as if it were yesterday; it was as if a strong person had gripped me to stop me from falling. I knew it was my heavenly Father. At my moment of utter weakness he held on to me – I was ready to chuck it in, but he gripped me.

Awareness of the gripping hand of God gives the overwhelming sense that you are watched over by him, and that he will not let you slip from his hand. This means you are confident that you belong to him.

I press on, that I may lay hold of that for which Christ Jesus has also laid hold of me. Brethren, I do not count myself to have apprehended; but one thing I do, forgetting those things which are behind and reaching forward to those things which are ahead, I press toward the goal for the prize of the upward call of God in Christ Jesus (Philippians 3:12–14, NKJV).

Paul clearly knew this gripping. He was gripped or laid hold of by Christ. He was a man turned on the road by such an encounter with God that he was gripped forever. But look, the gripping of God does something: it means that we too want to grip the very thing that we are called for. Christ laid hold of me so that I can lay hold of the very thing that he calls me to. When God has gripped you, something inside you will grip hold of the very 'life call' that you have. In these verses the inspiration is to press ahead with every fibre of energy and being. Paul does not look back, he does not turn and wonder what might have been; he is caught by the upward call of God in his life —he is pushing for God's prize for him.

I know what he must have felt like. I know that upward call. I know what it means to have a gripped heart, an intense, compulsive desire to do it God's way despite all the opportunities to do it my way. I think it is this upward call that makes us pilgrims rather than simply nomads.

Abraham had such an upward call. God gives a promise to make Abram a great nation, to bless him, to make him a blessing to others, to make him famous. In fact, Abram is promised that all the families on earth will be blessed through him.[3] When we get God's promise it moves us from a state of immobility and paralysis to a place of movement, journey and pilgrimage. This was not a promise for just one generation, rather there would be a passing on of the promise to the next generation —something which, to the short-term thinking of the modern mind, does not compute. We live in a society that values what can be experienced today – so all that matters is my generation. But that is clearly not the way that Father God sees it. He sees his people as generations upon generations.

Thankfully, Abram decides to move with the promise and he enters the land called Canaan, which is already occupied. He sets up an altar to the Lord in worship, but keeps travelling.[4] Abram is a prototype disciple; he leaves all in pursuit of something better. Just like the disciples Jesus called. They had to drop everything and follow him.[5] Most disciples nowadays are not called on to drop everything; we can have our cake and eat it. I think that this is a reason why the church fails to be missional. We preach a gospel that allows for duality, and we tend to reduce authentic faith to an insurance policy to secure eternal well-being. The word of the modern world is, 'It's all about me', and people lap it up. Yet most realise at a certain level that it is not about them —but until someone presents a real alternative they will go on consuming and experiencing whatever there is! But if the church can recapture the call to 'sold-out' discipleship, then perhaps the call of God will grip people to drop everything. It is the compelling call of God that turns our nomadic wanderings into pilgrimage. Abram became a man with a mission *confidently looking forward to a city with eternal foundations, a city designed and built by God.*[6]

EMBRACING THE IMPOSSIBLE

Faith is often about embracing the humanly impossible. Sure enough, you will face seemingly impossible barriers to the vision that God has placed in your heart. You are going to find sticking to your guns really hard. There is bound to come a moment when, frankly, it all looks incredibly bleak and totally impossible. God makes a number of promises to Abram. The one that may have seemed the hardest to believe was that Abram would have a son. Now remember that Abram and Sarai are ancient, so they had completely given up on the idea that they would conceive. It would have seemed ridiculous. In fact, Abram finds it so ridiculous that he laughs at God in disbelief.[7] One day, three men appear at Abraham's place. In fact, it is the Lord and two angels. Abraham rushes about making preparations for the visitors. Whilst having lunch, the mysterious visitors promise Abraham that in a year he and Sarah will have a child. Sarah is standing behind the door and hears them say this; she laughs as well. The men in the next room hear her laughing, but she lies and denies it!

The laughter of both Abraham and Sarah betrays a scepticism which is thoroughly modern. Cynical writers, broadcasters and influencers of our age would seek to marginalise and dismiss the people of faith as an irrelevant footnote in history. Faith is for the emotionally disabled, for people who need something outside themselves to prop up their feeble lives. Some would seek to push those of profound faith to the margins, suggesting that faith is no more than a recreational pursuit. We are expected to rationalise the supernatural to the satisfaction of humanists who, of course, can never be satisfied. When people of faith make mistakes they are paraded as hypocrites, particularly if they are high profile. Abraham and Sarah are held up to us as scriptural models of faith, yet they struggled to stay consistent. They sometimes failed to believe, yet the scriptures promote them as being faithful. Faith is the journey we are on; we go deeper into it and believe more of God as we go. You cannot just stop the faith journey in a moment of time and try to make sense out of it —it is to be the journey of our lives.

What I love about this passage is something it establishes about faith. Whatever is to be accomplished through faith may look so outlandishly ridiculous that it seems like a complete joke. The promise of God is not 'reasonable'; a life of faith is not comfortable; it cannot be squeezed into your ordinary everyday life. In no sense is this just recreational! No, the people of God are called to embrace the seeming 'impossibility' that becomes possible with God. We are supposed to take God's word and say, 'let's go for it', even if to do so seems completely stupid. In fact, I might be tempted to go so far as to say that if it isn't ridiculous the word 'vision' or 'dream' isn't big enough! Abraham and Sarah had been at this life of faith for some time, and they had embraced the normality of a barren existence. At one point they had settled for the fact that they had still not received what was promised, and it was laughable to think that this would change.

When we learn to live with a vision God has given us, the illusion that we have it all in hand – that we can do it by ourselves – is shattered. If you have received a heavenly vision, who ever said that you could achieve it all by yourself? The vision may seem impossible, but remember that, if it is birthed in heaven, God can do it.

Abraham and Sarah embraced the sterility of their

normality when they laughed at God's plan. Their barren condition was the place they had come from, and they had still not received the promise! It is easy to pick up the sterile past, particularly when things don't appear to be going as planned. But answer the question that the Lord asked Abraham: "Is anything too hard for the Lord?"[8] Of course, this concerns the matter in hand. There are certain things that God cannot do. He cannot do anything evil, for example. Whatever he does is always good. But what he can always do is to faithfully fulfil his word and his promises, as Abraham was to discover. If you deny God's power to fulfil what he has promised, you set up a barrier. You have decided that life in this universe is made up of things that are predictable, reliable, stable and, I would suggest, hopeless. You are in a situation and nothing can change it. But you could declare that nothing is impossible for God! Then endless possibilities open up; you break the bondage of a limiting mindset; you open yourself up to the freedom that comes from heaven. You have embraced the divine promise. Jesus teaches us that nothing is impossible for believing people.[9] Depending on God to fulfil his word and bring to fruition the vision he has entrusted to you will keep you hungry, on track, and fixed in the right direction.

TESTING

Any look at Abraham's life would seem incomplete if we did not at least touch on the testing of his vision.[10] God asks Abraham to take Isaac to the land of Moriah, and sacrifice him on the mountain God will show him. So without a word of protest or argument they set off with two servants.

By this point in Abraham's pilgrimage he is in a different place. He is ready to be addressed by God and to obey him. He has been told to go to an unknown place before, so this is okay. He isn't going to argue with God; he had learned the hard way that when God speaks to him he has to believe, no protest. He knew that God knew what he was doing. Although God's ways appear incomprehensible and mysterious, Abraham was not going to dispute God's directions this time.

God is the tester. He will take Abraham on a journey to uncover the depth of his faith —a journey into the unknown. The reader is left in no doubt that this strange request by God was intended to test Abraham's faith. The actual death of Isaac was not, in fact, God's intention. But Abraham was totally in the dark about God's real intention. This was an indescribably painful trial.

DOES GOD TEST?

This was a world not unlike our own where the worship of Yahweh was one option; there were other gods that vied for people's attention. So we are shown that God tests a believer's devotion. Could God today test our hearts, our motives, our worship? How easily we turn to the gods of pleasure, comfort and personal fulfilment. Would God actually test *you* for his purposes? Are the 'gods' of the twenty-first century world not seductively attractive to many? Do they seem less demanding than the true and living God? The command of God to sacrifice Isaac seems to be opposed to the promise that Isaac would spawn a nation. Things that God says may offend human logic. Ultimately, we must face the fact that God is sovereign; even when his commands to us seem absurd, with heaven's insight they make divine logic.

On the third day, Abraham sees the mountain. He takes his promised son to worship God. He is confident that they will both return,[11] reasoning that God would raise his son from the dead. Isaac himself carries the firewood, and Abraham the fire and knife.

Worship here is an act of ultimate sacrifice. Worship isn't just a musical feast on a Sunday; it is our sacrifice to God. Here, it looked as though the worship of God was going to cost Abraham his son and the promise. He didn't doubt that God would do what he said he would do, so he didn't really try and understand. He just came to the conclusion that it would take another miracle —here was another opportunity for God to show his faithfulness. Sacrifice is built into the scriptural narrative, and is especially prominent at times of devotion, thankfulness, celebration and forgiveness. Without an understanding of the need for sacrifice we cannot comprehend the need for Christ's death.

'Hey, father, where is the sheep for the offering?' asks Isaac. The reply is, 'God will provide.' This is really the punchline of the story. God provides. We know the end —God comes up with the goods. Is Abraham just trying to shut Isaac up? No, this is a man confident in his God. He has learned how to walk on a journey of faith, and once again he is going on a journey of faith with his son —faith in action.

The sacrificial altar is built, and obediently, without any protest, Isaac lies on the altar! Abraham raises the knife . . . . Surely you want to shout with me, 'Isaac, get off the altar!' Stupid, trusting Isaac . . . . But he knows his father; he knows he is the son of promise, so he trusts Abraham, even when all the signals seem bad.

Abraham, what are you thinking? Did he think: I must be obedient, God will raise him up?

SACRIFICE

Trusting in his Father, Jesus went to the cross, even when Father was silent. Jesus cries out for his Father to intervene, but death comes, and with it the greatest act of sacrifice of all time. When God is testing our faith, it will demand sacrifice. Sacrifice is part of the journey of faith: sacrifice of money, sacrifice of security, sacrifice of career choices. Society applauds the sacrifice of athletes and war heroes, yet we avoid personal inconvenience at all costs. We are happy to sacrifice if it means we can still have and do whatever we want. Gritty, real, adventurous faith is built on the notion of sacrifice. There will be sacrifice in the journey of faith. Of course, our sacrifice does not earn us access to God. Only the one sacrifice once made by Jesus on the cross is effectual. The sort of sacrifice we are thinking about here, though, is sometimes called 'surrender' —it is part of the inevitable outworking of our faith, a willingness to lay everything on the line.

A voice from heaven intervenes.

"Abraham, Abraham."

"Here I am."

"Don't do it. I now know that you fear God. Because you would not even withhold your son for me."

They saw a lamb caught in the bush and sacrificed that

instead. They named the place 'The Lord will provide', and God confirms the promise again.

The test is over, and Abraham has passed. He bore it well. In God's sovereign heavenly plan there was a test of faith for Abraham, and the solution at the right moment. We often call on God's provision, but are reluctant to make whatever sacrifice may be needed. Yet our preparedness to sacrifice what has become precious to us is what is often needed in the journey of faith. Perhaps we find it odd that a God of unfailing love could test us? Is it a consumer religion that wants a provider God while rejecting the idea of a God who tests faith? Is it reasonable that God tests? REASONABLE! God has revealed all we need to know for our salvation, but our reason will never be enough. His ways are supernatural, not restricted to what our human reason can grasp.

So be truly glad. There is wonderful joy ahead, even though you have to endure many trials for a little while. These trials will show that your faith is genuine. It is being tested as fire tests and purifies gold—though your faith is far more precious than mere gold. So when your faith remains strong through many trials, it will bring you much praise and glory and honor on the day when Jesus Christ is revealed to the whole world (1 Peter 1:6-7, NLT).

Testing from God is to strengthen us, to purify us, to make us stronger. God is not vindictive or cruel. Faith is trusting in the power of the true and living God who brings resurrection. Faith is trusting in the God who can make stuff out of nothing. Jesus was crucified and resurrected.

If you try to hang on to your life, you will lose it. But if you give up your life for my sake and for the sake of the Good News, you will save it (Mark 8:35, NLT).

Testing will be part of the pilgrimage of faith. When you are finally pursuing the vision from God, there will be God tests along the way to ensure that the vision remains heavenly.

BEING A HERO OF FAITH

So, Abraham heads off into the adventure and gets everything that God promised. Um . . . I don't think so. Hebrews says they all died without receiving what was promised.[12] What! What is the point of that? They saw it all from a distance and welcomed it. They got a taste and a down payment, but didn't actually receive what was promised. We see that faith captured their hearts, minds and imaginations. They were not consumed by a physical answer to prayer and promise, rather they were captured by the eternal fulfilment of the promise.

Now don't get me wrong, we need to hear God, believe and go for it, expecting delivery of the promised goods, but I am going to depart this world with vision and expectation still brimming, stuff that I want to do that my spiritual sons will have to pick up and fulfil for me. I can't imagine anything worse than to find myself at eighty-five just reliving my success or failure. No, I want to keep on with the vision and the dream that I am believing will be fulfilled, even if I do not see it all happen myself.

Implicit in this passage is the idea of the baton of faith being passed from one generation to the next. We don't only live it out for our generation but also for every generation to come. Relay runners don't run, stop, pass on the baton and then go and have a cup of coffee. No, they run and the second runner runs with them for a while to pick up the pace, then the baton is passed and the first runner keeps running for a bit. When they do drop out, they are as interested in the result of the race as the final runner who passes the finishing line. It is as much the first runner's victory as the last runner's victory. Now you may be reading this and be the first runner with a particular vision, or you may be a runner in a long line of people carrying the vision for what you are pursuing. The reward is not a 'gold medal' as soon as the vision becomes reality but a (much better) heavenly reward.

Hebrews 11 reminds us of all those faithful men and women who have gone before us —and you have an important part to play in the same 'relay race'! You may well achieve the vision, but there is normally a list of faithful heroes who have gone before you.

In the team that I have the privilege and honour to lead, when we have moments of failure, of letting each other down, I say that we are in this for the long run. I have no interest in short-term success. What matters is lasting victory that is sustained over years, and passed on to the next bunch of leaders that God calls. We need to be in the 'gallery of the faithful' so that we can continue the unbroken line of faith into this generation.

We need today a faithful generation of believers to pick up the baton, and get running. Our attitude has to shift from survival to overcoming, from just getting through to getting on top, from being the man to being the men.

Here in Hebrews we have story after story to demonstrate the truth that God is in the business of speaking to us continually. He plants ideas, visions, goals and passions into us, things that bring us alive, things of which we can say, 'I was made for this'. We need to be ready to receive what he is saying to us. When we do this we are generating faith. The very action of listening to his words, and deciding to believe those words, solidifies something in our lives. This is faith with which we begin to trust. Just like concrete when it is set, we can stand on faith and step out on it, no matter what is happening around us, because faith really doesn't depend on the environment we are in. If you get this principle, the dream that is on the inside of you is one more step further towards becoming a reality.

IT IS BIGGER THAN YOU!

A self-consumed society tries very hard to reduce everything to the 'here and now'. We have to fight very hard as the people of God to reject this. We are of generations of people who have decided to live this life of faith. As such, we need to do our part. Your part is to grip the vision that God has placed in your heart, no matter how impossible it may seem, no matter what the consequences, no matter how risky—and live it out. There is no certainty that you will even realise the vision in your heart. You may have to pass the vision on to the next generation. If every believer started to live the God-given vision that is in him or her, we would become a force unparalleled in the world:

> • *A people of imagination in a world that needs a picture to grasp hold of, a new identity in which to find itself.*
>
> • *A people of initiative who are making a difference in a land where lethargy reigns.*
>
> • *A people of adventure who will awaken a love of God in the nation.*
>
> • *A people of faith, believing what sometimes seems humanly 'impossible' but is possible with God; displaying supernatural reality to the sceptical world.*

Come on, church! See the vision and start to live the heavenly way!

NOTES

Chapter 2
1   Ephesians 4:16; 1 Corinthians 12:12–28
2   Hebrews 11:11
3   Genesis 18:11–15
4   Genesis 17:17
5   Genesis 21:1–7
6   Jeremiah 29:11
7   Psalm 37:4

Chapter 3
1   Acts 6:1–7
2   Acts 6:5
3   Acts 6:8
4   Acts 6:15
5   Acts 7:1–53
6   Acts 7:55
7   2 Corinthians 5:20
8   Philippians 3:20
9   Philippians 1:19–26
10   *Through the Bible Day by Day*
11   Acts 2:11
12   Acts 2:19
13   Acts 2:43
14   Acts 3:10
15   Acts 3:1–10
16   Acts 2:41; 5:14; 6:17

Chapter 4
1   Matthew 3:1
2   Matthew 4:17
3   Mark 6:45–50
4   Philippians 3:20
5   Matthew 6:20
6   Hebrews 11:1
7   Colossians 3:2
8   Luke 11:1–4
9   See *Amplified Bible*

Chapter 5
1   Revelation 3:14–22
2   Revelation 3:18
3   Isaiah 55:1
4   Matthew 5:6
5   John 6:35
6   John 4:7–15
7   John 7:37–39
8   Revelation 3:7–13
9   cf. Isaiah 22:22
10   Ephesians 1:3
11   Matthew 6:20

¹² Psalm 78:23
¹³ Malachi 2:17–3:5; 4
¹⁴ Malachi 4:6
¹⁵ Ephesians 1:20
¹⁶ Ephesians 2:6
¹⁷ Luke 10:20
¹⁸ John 14:2
¹⁹ Ephesians 3:10
²⁰ Ephesians 6:13

Chapter 6
¹ Cf. Genesis 4:2–5
² Genesis 5:21–24
³ Hebrews 11:6
⁴ Genesis 6:9
⁵ Genesis 12
⁶ Hebrews 11:10
⁷ Genesis 15:6

Chapter 7
¹ John 10:11
² Hebrews 13:17
³ Hebrews 13:7
⁴ 1 Corinthians 1:27; 2 Corinthians 12:10
⁵ Ephesians 6:12
⁶ 1 Corinthians 13:9
⁷ 1 Corinthians 13:12
⁸ Genesis 41
⁹ Genesis 20:3
¹⁰ Daniel 2
¹¹ Matthew 27:19
¹² Genesis 28:10–22
¹³ Genesis 37:5–11
¹⁴ Genesis 31:24
¹⁵ Matthew 2:12
¹⁶ Matthew 2:19, 22
¹⁷ Judges 7
¹⁸ Matthew 1:20
¹⁹ Numbers 12:6
²⁰ Acts 2:17, Joel 2:28
²¹ 1 Kings 3:5
²² For a comprehensive examination and training
in dream interpretation I would recommend
John Paul Jackson's Streams International:
www.streamsministries.com
²³ 1 Chronicles 21:9; 2 Chronicles 9:29
²⁴ Ezekiel 3:14, 16
²⁵ Ezekiel 3:14
²⁶ Acts 1:10
²⁷ Acts 5:19

28 Acts 8:26
29 Hebrews 1:14
30 1 Kings 19:5–9
31 Acts 27:23
32 Luke 1:11
33 Luke 1:28
34 Luke 2:9–15
35 Daniel 8:16
36 Daniel 9:22
37 Daniel 10:11, 18
38 Hebrews 2:2
39 Acts 7:53

Chapter 8

1 John Eldredge, *Wild at Heart*
   (Thomas Nelson, 2001)
2 Genesis 11:27–32
3 Joshua 24:2
4 Acts 7:2–4
5 The original Hebrew spelling has a slight variant.
6 Matthew 25:14–30
7 Galatians 5:7
8 Hebrews 12:1
9 Not my words; by Erwin McManus —if you haven't read it,
   read *The Barbarian Way*. Great book!

Chapter 9

1 Philippians 3:14
2 Hebrews 11:1
3 Romans 4:16
4 Genesis 12:2–3
5 Genesis 13:14–17
6 Genesis 15:5
7 Genesis 17
8 Acts 15:11
9 2 Timothy 2:1
10 2 Corinthians 12:9
11 Ephesians 6:13
12 Proverbs 13:12
13 Acts 23:6
14 Colossians 1:23
15 Romans 5:2
16 1 Thessalonians 5:8
17 Ephesians 4:4
18 Titus 1:2; 3:7
19 Acts 26:6-7
20 2 Thessalonians 2:16; Titus 2:13; 1 Peter 1:3;
   Hebrews 7:19
21 Romans 8:24f
22 2 Corinthians 3:12

Chapter 10
1   Romans 4:1
2   Romans 4:12
3   Genesis 12:2f
4   Genesis 12:4–9
5   Mark 10:28
6   Hebrews 11:10
7   Genesis 17:17
8   Genesis 18:14, NIV
9   Matthew 17:20
10 Genesis 22
11 Hebrews 11:19
12 Hebrews 11:13

RESOURCES
CDs FROM BATH CITY CHURCH (prices include UK p & p)

KAIROS
Stewart Keiller   £9   CD-006-KAI
Time passing you by? Missed the moment? Redeem the time and appreciate the seasons of the soul.

FAITH WORKS
Stewart Keiller & Stephen Wood   £11   CD-012-FAI
How to take everyday decisions from a place of confidence in what God has said to you.

MAKING A DIFFERENCE
Stewart Keiller & Stephen Wood   £11   CD-005-DIF
God has a plan for you: he wants you to fulfil the dreams he has given you, using the power of the Holy Spirit to help you live it.

NO GUTS NO GLORY!
Stewart Keiller   £11   CD-011-GUT
Challenges men to be the men God created them to be, and to do what God has called them to do.

THE ANCHOR OF HOPE
Stewart Keiller   £5   CD-010-HOP
Feeling tossed about by the storms of life? Find out how to lay hold of hope —the anchor we need.

WHOM SHALL I FEAR?
Stewart Keiller   £5   CD-009-FEA
Afraid? The threat from terror? Your circumstances? Access the resources of heaven and find a place of peace.

To order online, visit: **www.bathcitychurch.org.uk**
Telephone +44(0)1225 463556   Fax +44(0)1225 460651